Dion Fortune's

# THE COSMIC DOCTRINE

*By the same author:*

*Occult study*

APPLIED MAGIC and ASPECTS OF OCCULTISM
ESOTERIC ORDERS AND THEIR WORK and TRAINING AND WORK OF THE INITIATE
ESOTERIC PHILOSOPHY OF LOVE AND MARRIAGE and PROBLEM OF PURITY
GLASTONBURY — AVALON OF THE HEART
MYSTICAL QABALAH
PSYCHIC SELF-DEFENCE
SANE OCCULTISM and PRACTICAL OCCULTISM IN DAILY LIFE
THROUGH THE GATES OF DEATH and SPIRITUALISM IN THE LIGHT OF OCCULT SCIENCE

*Occult fiction*

DEMON LOVER
GOAT-FOOT GOD
MOON MAGIC
SEA PRIESTESS
SECRETS OF DR TAVERNER
WINGED BULL

# Dion Fortune's THE COSMIC DOCTRINE

THE AQUARIAN PRESS

This edition first published 1988



British Library Cataloguing in Publication Data

Fortune, Dion
Dion Fortune's The cosmic doctrine —
New ed.
1. Occultism
I. Title II. The cosmic doctrine
133 BF1411

ISBN 0-85030-733-7

*The Aquarian Press is part of the Thorsons Publishing Group, Wellingborough, Northamptonshire, NN8 2RQ, England*

Printed in Great Britain by Biddles Limited, Guildford, Surrey

3 5 7 9 10 8 6 4 2

# Contents

The works of the late Dion Fortune were written a long time ago and since then a great deal more has been understood and realized so that many of the ideas then expressed are not now necessarily acceptable. Also, much of what she wrote was written from the viewpoint of the psychic. Psychism is simply one type of inner awareness and there are other types at least as valid and as common. Non-psychic readers, therefore, can translate experience in terms of psychic imagery into terms of their own inner awareness.

The publication of these books continues at present because there is still much of value in them and because they act as valuable pointers to seekers.

Details of the aims and work of the Society of the Inner Light, founded by Dion Fortune, may be obtained by writing (with postage please) to the Secretary at 38 Steele's Road, London NW3 4RG, England.

# Introduction

This volume of teaching was received from the Inner Planes during 1923 and 1924. The one who gave it is a human being evolved to a very high level. The Personality of his last incarnation is known but is not revealed, but it may be said that it was of a world-famous philosopher and teacher. In the terminology which is used in esotericism this individual is one of the 'Greater Masters'.

The object of these teachings is to induce a deeper understanding of Cosmic Law, and to expand consciousness that it may lift thoughts to the source from which they issued. These teachings will also be found to form a basis upon which considerable esoteric knowledge can be built, and to contain the explanation of much that has hitherto been inaccessible to the general reader. On account of the vastness of the conception, however, which is beyond the limitations of our concrete minds, it has been necessary to resort to the extensive use of metaphor.

The reader is advised to persevere in his efforts to gain the utmost from these teachings by study and meditation.

The word 'Master', used in esotericism, is not one I should have chosen since it has the association of 'master and servant' as well as the association implied here of 'master and pupil'. However, we inherit the expressions standardized by those who revived the search for the 'Ancient Wisdom' in the West and must make the best of them though it is possible and desirable to discard foreign words (usually Sanscrit or Hindu) as much as possible and use instead our own English equivalents. 'Logos' is retained in the text since it has a clearly defined application whereas 'God' tends to be rather vague and difficult to dissociate from sectarian convictions.

Concerning the 'Masters' or Inner Plane Adepti I should like to make it clear that these are of a far higher stage of development than those discarnate communicators who describe the 'summerlands', personal 'heaven-worlds', of their own subjective Inner-Plane state. The latter have little of value to tell the average well-educated man; the former have a very great deal but usually work only through carefully chosen and highly trained individuals save, of course, for the 'contacts' each of us may succeed in making for himself and which result in intuitional apprehension. This, however, should be treated with great caution and unless the matter given is sound should not be taken as genuine.

The Inner Plane Adepti have touched on the question of their state and conditions from time to time and three extracts are given below which may be of value to the reader unfamiliar with the subject. These great intelligences have developed beyond the need to incarnate and all the experiences of their lives on earth have been absorbed in essence into their present make-up. Needless to say they are no longer incarnate and the tales of their living on the earth in remote places are quite groundless: to anyone who knows what a 'Master' is by development it is commonsense to realize that such do not at present live on earth. There are, of course, high adepts (highly developed and illuminated men) but these are not yet 'Masters.' It may be that in future as evolution proceeds 'illuminati' of the grade of Masters may remain on earth instead of passing on to the Inner Planes, in full contact with Inner and Outer Planes in order to accomplish certain work as long as the physical vehicle remains efficient.

> 'If a man sets out to look for the Path he evinces a desire. That desire will be noted by those who watch on the Inner Planes and he will be "assigned to a class" according to his temperament. After he has gone a certain way under that tuition he will be put in the care of what is called a "guide"; this is the first work souls are employed on when they take up work on this side. The guide will try to impress the teaching he wishes to convey on the soul of his pupil by telepathy, and the pupil must try to catch what is "said".
>
> Later the pupil will be put into touch with one of the Lesser Masters and be one of a number of pupils for whom that Master is responsible. A guide has only one pupil at a time but a Master has many. As the pupil advances further he will be passed to Masters of higher grade. His problem will always be to catch what his Master says. The higher the grade of Master the further he is away from Earth.'

> 'What are the Masters? Human beings like yourselves, but older. They are not Gods, nor Angels, nor Elementals but are those individuals who have achieved and completed the same task as you have set yourselves. What you are now, they were once. What they are now, you can be.
>
> Have you so little belief in the survival of bodily death that you cannot conceive of the existence of the Masters? Have you so little belief in the

doctrine of evolution that you cannot conceive of human beings as greatly superior to yourselves as you are to the animals? Have you so little knowledge of the power of the mind that you do not believe in the possibility of communication between you and them? If there is nothing higher than yourselves what hope have you? And if you accept the possibility why should you not try it? And if you try for it why should you not expect that your first achievements will be rudimentary and imperfect and inaccurate? But if you never make a beginning you will never arrive at completion. You must be content to speak in broken tones before you can speak fluently. If you do not so essay you will never learn to speak. We shall teach you the language.'

'The Masters as you picture them are all "imagination". Note well that I did not say that the Masters were imagination; I said "*The Masters as you picture them*". What we are you cannot realize and it is a waste of time to try to do so but you can imagine us on the astral plane and we can contact you through your imagination, and although your mental picture is not real or actual, the results of it are real and actual.

The Masters as they are supposed to be in popular would-be esoteric thought are pure fiction; but as long as you are a "concrete" consciousness you will have to use the astral to reach the abstract. It is the laws of astral thought form that are taught in occult science.

The difference between the man who touches astral imagination only, and the man who by astral imagination touches spiritual actualities, is that the former in his concepts can rise no higher than the astral imagination the latter has in his soul spiritual realization and aspiration which he brings through into "brain consciousness" by means of the astral imagination.'

The Master responsible for the teaching set out in this volume prefaced his first lecture by the following foreword: 'I am interested and concerned in teaching and I have always been concerned with students. It is not the easiest thing to give an ordered cosmogony and Science of Man and I may well be somewhat disconnected; but it is enough if you have the matter. There are various textbooks of the Ancient Wisdom extant but those books are mainly for those following their particular line of development because books speak not only to the conscious mind but also to the sub-conscious. They lift thought to the source of the concepts.

Knowledge falls into two divisions—the record of facts and the explanation thereof. Knowledge can only consist of that which is present in the mind. That which does not enter the mind cannot be known. Therefore you can only know that which you have senses to interpret to you. As new senses open up more planes of existence can be known. There is, however, a limit to the knowledge possible—the finite. Perception ceases at the barrier of manifestation. Of that which lies beyond we can only know by analogy'.

In such abstruse matters allowance must be made by each reader for difficulties of communication and it must be kept in mind that the communicator is trying to find the most suitable metaphors to convey transcendental ideas. *Each one should use his imagination and intuition in reading, for this is not a simple statement of the solution of an elementary theorem but an endeavour to convey very abstract ideas in reasonably concrete form* to those those still in incarnation by one who has long finished with the need for a physical body.

1.

# The Dawn of Manifestation

The Unmanifest is pure existence. We cannot say of it that it is *not*. Although it is not manifest, it *is*. IT is the source from which all arises. IT is the only 'Reality'. IT alone is substance. IT alone is stable; all else is an appearance and a becoming. Of this Unmanifest we can only say 'IT IS'. IT is the verb 'to be' turned back upon itself. IT is a state of pure 'being', without qualities and without history. All we can say of IT is that it is not anything that we know, for if we know anything it must be in manifestation for us to know it, and if it is in manifestation that proves that it is not unmanifest. The Unmanifest is the Great Negation; at the same time IT is the infinite potency which has not occurred. It is best conceived of under the image of interstellar space.

In these occult teachings you will be given certain images, under which you are instructed to think of certain things. These images are not descriptive but symbolic, *and are designed to train the mind, not to inform it*. Therefore, you may think of the Unmanifest as interstellar space; and of the Logos as a Sun surrounded by Its Solar System of Planets; and of the emanations of the Logos as Rays. The Unmanifest is the only Unity. Manifestation begins when duality occurs.

The prime duality is 'space' and 'movement'. The first manifestation was a current in space—the metaphor I must use may convey nothing to your mind. All I can say is that 'space' was moving: you will find these words the clue to much.

Now, when space moves it has this peculiar quality—being frictionless it never loses momentum, but continues to flow. When space moves, two forces are at work:

(a) The force which causes it to move, being the desire of space for momentum.

(b) The force which has hitherto caused it not to move, being the desire of space for inertia.

These two factors are present in all motion, but the desire for movement, being the stronger, overcomes the desire for inertia, and the desire for inertia continues as a check upon the movement. Therefore the movement is pulled upon slightly. That is why there is no such thing as a straight line in the Cosmos. All movement, therefore, has a slight curve in its projection; therefore, eventually it returns to the point whence it started, and forms a spinning ring.

Now, the prime movement is just a flowing of space that returns after long aeons whence it started, and then renews its journey. This sets up a spinning belt of enormous circumference. This belt spins in one plane for immense aeons of time; spins with a changeless spinning. But its tendency is to communicate its motion to the space about it, which leads more space to flow into the spinning. (All this, remember, is metaphor). The spinning in one plane continues until the stresses which it generates evoke a new movement, and a second current in space is set up at right angles to the first, and the same process is repeated.

We have now two spinning planes, the one within the other, and it is worthy of note that the second plane forms outside the first, and is therefore larger in diameter.

For countless aeons these planes spin at right angles to each other, and the whole of evolution turns upon the difference in size between the planes. When the larger has attained the same speed as the smaller and older, it commences to attract one aspect of it, the consequence being that the older circle is drawn towards the newer.

Now, the first circle must be conceived of as having an upper and a lower surface. The upper surface of the outflowing arc may be conceived of as positive, and the lower as negative. The reverse being the case in the inflowing arc.

Likewise with the second circle to arise.

These circles are mutually attracting and repelling each other; so that you can conceive the upper surface of the outflowing arc (of the first circle) being positive, rising up towards its complementary aspect in the second circle, and the lower surface in the returning arc pressing downwards, so that you get a second movement imparted to the spinning disc. When this secondary movement has completed its first circuit and sets up its steady revolution, the new Cosmos is in being. That is the prime beginning of a Cosmos expressed in the nearest approximate metaphor.

The secondary spin of the first circuit is the Ring-Pass-Not, and the circuit of the second formation is that sphere which sets a bound to

Chaos. On the outer sphere there is also a secondary derivation, and though a spinning circle of motion, it represents, for that Cosmos, the prime stillness, the immobility in which it is rooted, it is the thrust-block of the force of the Cosmos, that which resists, which alone enables momentum to be achieved, and you may call it the Ring-Chaos—the 'Prime Evil'. It is evolved from the reaction of the prime force in order to take its thrust. It spins at right angles to the prime spin. It counteracts it. It was the attraction of the Ring-Chaos which set the Ring-Cosmos in its second motion, and so formed that secondary spin which we call the Ring-Pass-Not, the prime limitation. Therefore, at base, it is the Prime Evil which enables the Cosmos to come into being.

# 2.

# The Forces of (Negative) Evil

Before proceeding further, we must explain the concept of evil. Referring back you will perceive that the first movement gave rise to a secondary movement, according to the laws of reaction, and that the second movement, in opposition to the first, produced stability. It is always the function of opposition to produce stability. Evil in this sense is only the opposition to the angle of the prime current. It is a secondary spin which arises as a reaction to the primary. You will hear more of the true concept of evil later. Evil imparts finiteness—limitation, and therefore concentrates; and evil must be properly understood, for then its forces can be used in their proper functions as a thrust-block. It is when the position is reversed and an attempt is made to work the forces of the Ring-Chaos dynamically that evil arises in the popular sense of the term. Evil must be conceived of esoterically as a limitation which enables pressure to be raised—as the rejection which enables concentration to be achieved.

I will give you an example. 'Sensuality', you say, 'is evil and to be avoided', therefore the life-forces are concentrated on the upper planes because a certain expression is denied them. If there were no denial but the free flow of perfect harmony there would be no concentration, and therefore no work. You cannot get work from steam rising from an open vessel. This function of evil needs to be very carefully understood. You will always get your push-off from evil. Every advance to a higher plane is a reaction to evil. If there were no evil, there would be no point in improvement, therefore there would be no growth, no evolution.

To recapitulate the teaching: We have the prime spin of the Ring-Cosmos; the reaction giving rise to the Ring-Chaos; the attraction of the Ring-Chaos inducing a secondary spin in the Ring-Cosmos which forms the Ring-Pass-Not.

Now, that movement in the Ring-Cosmos, spinning in one plane and rotating while it spins, as if upon an axis, sets the bounds beyond which the creatures of that sphere cannot pass even in thought. But this sphere is encircled by two lines of force—the Ring-Cosmos and the Ring-Chaos, rotating at right angles to each other. The rotation of the Ring-Cosmos is the source of force from which evolution draws its momentum; and the rotation of the Ring-Chaos is the source of force from which devolution draws its power.

Evolution is a thrust from the circumference towards the centre.

Devolution, or dissolution, is a suction into outer space.

The Ring-Chaos does not belong to the sphere it encircles, but to outer space. That is an important point in connection with it.

The Ring-Cosmos has its desires turned towards the sphere it encircles.

The Ring-Chaos has its desires turned towards the space that encircles it.

The Ring-Cosmos seeks to extend the centre.

The Ring-Chaos seeks to extend the circumference.

The Ring-Cosmos tends to solidify by contraction.

The Ring-Chaos tends to return to the Unmanifest whence it arose, and therefore, if its influence were unchecked, to reduce the sphere it encircles to nothingness.

The Ring-Cosmos, if its influence were unchecked, would be static in the immediate present.

These two influences are the source of all the force in the Cosmos. The Ring-Cosmos, because it concretes—builds up. The Ring-Chaos, because it diffuses—never grows.

Now, these two Rings we will call Good and Evil; Life and Death; Light and Darkness; Spirit and Matter; Being and Not-Being; God and Devil, because each of these potencies has its root in its respective Ring. But let it be clearly conceived that the Ring 'Good' and the Ring 'Evil' are not 'good' and 'evil' as you understand these terms, but merely spinning circles of force at right angles to each other, and therefore in opposition; and it is merely the angle of the first to arise which is called 'good', and the angle in opposition to the prime plane which is called 'evil', and it might well be that in another Cosmos, the first plane would begin to spin at another angle—the angle of your 'evil'. It would still be 'good' to its Cosmos, because 'good' and 'evil' do not depend upon any angle or plane, but are simply relative to each other. The first force to arise is called 'good' because, from it, arises the line of force called evolution. All subsequent secondary forces are measured by that standard. In so far as they move in the same angle they are reckoned to be 'good'.

In so far as they approach to a right angle, they are reckoned to be in opposition, and are called 'evil'. Evil is simply that which is moving in the opposite direction to evolution. Evil is that which approached the plane of movement of the Ring-Chaos, and therefore tends to revert to the Unmanifest. All evil that builds up with a universe is attracted towards the Ring-Chaos and is self-destroyed, because the very idea 'evil' implies a force which tends to non-existence.

So you can conceive of evil under two aspects:

(a) That which enables you to lock up the forces of good by opposition, and so secure stability—a foothold; evil enables you to get a purchase on space.

(b) Evil, if allowed to function unopposed, is the Scavenger of the Gods. Therefore, said a Great One, 'Resist not evil'. When you resist evil you lock up good, you lock up the force of good which holds the evil inert. This serves no useful purpose, unless you have a superabundance of good which shall stand upon the platform thus formed and leap up from it to greater heights. Therefore, it is not enough to meet hate with love—evil with good; this is the course of the ignorant, and the reason why exoteric religion has made so little impression in the world. You must meet hate with hate sufficiently to cause a locking-up of the force. You must hate the hate, and, having rendered evil inert by opposition, the love can take its stand upon the firm platform and use it as a thrust-block.

Therefore, you only oppose evil when you wish to do constructive work—when you wish to make something new. You never oppose the evil which you mean to destroy. You make a vacuum round it. You prevent opposition from touching it. Then, being unopposed, it is free to follow the laws of its own nature, which is to join the motion of the Ring-Chaos. It, therefore, passes out to the periphery of the universe till it meets the spin of the Ring-Pass-Not which it cannot get through, but it has gone to a place of such primitive simplicity that it is resolved into its own elements, and these elements are drawn into the attraction of the nearest motion, which is the nature of the Ring-Cosmos, which is the nature of good.

Therefore, evil, when unopposed, resolves itself into the undifferentiated raw material of existence—the first form of manifestation. It ceases to be organized. It ceases to have qualities. It starts afresh at the beginning, transmuted through neutrality into good.

It is the spin of these two Rings which gives the influences that play upon creation.

You are now in a position to know why the mystery of evil is the secret of the Initiates,* because when you understand evil it is exceedingly useful. But the undisciplined man, if he knew the usefulness and goodness of evil, would use it dynamically on the positive side of its manifestation, not statically by availing himself of its negative qualities as does the Initiate.

**Corrigendum**

The following comes from an authoritative source to remove any confusion from the name 'Negative Evil':

'To call the Ring-Chaos "Negative Evil" is unsatisfactory. The word "Evil" should not have been used as it can cause confusion to many and is liable to be misunderstood even by the more versed in our terminology. Without the change and tension caused by growth the Cosmos could not progress to its own finality. The Ring-Chaos is not alien to the Ring-Cosmos but proceeds from it and is in eternal association with it.

The interworking of the two Rings is like the conscious and sub-conscious mind of man. If the Ring-Chaos can be considered at all as "Negative" it should be as "Negative Good". The Absolute is Itself Law—what is in opposition is not necessarily at enmity.'

* Where, in this book, the word 'Initiate' is spelt with a capital 'I' an illuminated adept is to be understood.

3.

# The Twelve Rays and the Seven Cosmic Planes

You have to conceive of the Cosmos, in its primal aspect, as consisting of three spinning movements. All that is, is nothing but movement—movement in space—pure movement; and the prime movement which gives rise to all that is, commences before there is anything to move. The Cosmos is bounded by that movement which is called the Ring-Pass-Not. But besides the Ring-Pass-Not there are movements in two directions. These are the Rings Cosmos and Chaos, 'good' and 'evil', and they are the sources of the forces which are known to you by these names. But though these forces influence that which is within the Ring-Pass-Not, that which is within this Ring cannot pass beyond it.

These three movements are the three 'primaries' of the Cosmos—the first Trinity. That is why the Supreme Being in this manifestation is always conceived of as a Trinity and three is the fundamental number. Everything in the end is reducible to these three influences. Whatever subsequent stresses arise may be analysed into the balancing of these three forces:

(a) The force of the Ring-Cosmos, which tends towards the centre.

(b) The force of the Ring-Chaos which tends towards outer space.

(c) The force of the Ring-Pass-Not which holds the balance between them and prevents either of these forces from going to extremes.

The Ring-Pass-Not, however, is derived from the Ring-Cosmos, and therefore partakes of its nature rather than of that of the Ring-Chaos.

The Ring-Chaos must always be thought of as having its affinity with the outer space of the Unmanifest, and a tendency to return to unmanifestation. It looks towards the past and ever seeks the conditions of the past.

The Ring-Cosmos endeavours to focus, as the Ring-Chaos endeavours to diffuse. The tendency of the Ring-Cosmos is towards the future.

The Ring-Chaos can never build anything, because whatever forces it may originate diffuse unconfined into outer space. But the Ring-Cosmos, in conjunction with the Ring-Pass-Not, conserves its forces. For the forces which the Ring-Cosmos radiates into that space within its circumference cannot pass out again because they are confined by the influences of the Ring-Pass-Not. Therefore, they act and interact among themselves, producing ever greater and greater elaborations of influences.

Let us now return to the point in time when the Ring-Pass-Not has completed its first revolution, and the Cosmos is in being.

Any form of force, when it has reached the maximum momentum of its type of movement, gives rise to secondary movements which serve to carry off the excess of force which it is generating; for force begets force when moving under frictionless conditions.

The prime activity is MOVEMENT.

The second activity is LIGHT.

The third activity is SOUND.

The movement of the Ring-Cosmos sets up secondary swirls within the area of its influence; its tendency is to draw more and more space into its spin. It cannot extend externally because it is limited by the sphere of the Ring-Chaos; it therefore extends itself internally, so that the spinning belt finally becomes a spinning disc with the centre immobile.

The spinning disc, being rotated by the secondary movement which is the Ring-Pass-Not, becomes the spinning sphere.

The interaction of the two forms of movement is naturally neutralizing, consequently there is a break-up of the simple movement of the disc into a series of compromises. The chief point of activity ceases to be the circumference and becomes the centre.

Though the Ring-Cosmos, the Ring-Chaos, and the Ring-Pass-Not each continue in one plane, and spin in their own place, the synthesis of their movements give rise to a series of revolving radii. These radii are the Rays.

You must conceive of them as a series of revolving spirals linking the centre to the circumference and see:

(a) The influence of the Ring-Chaos in the force which causes the outgoing current to flow towards the periphery.

(b) The influence of the Ring-Cosmos in the force which causes the current to flow towards the centre.

(c) The centre is the synthesis of all the forces, and the balancing of them.

It will be perceived then, that upon the Cosmic plane the Rays give rise to the Central Sun.

We have now arrived at the point when, in addition to the three great 'primaries' which are strictly external to the Cosmos they have generated, we have a purely cosmic movement—the movement of the flowing Rays—the Rays that flow out and return.

Now these Rays—these circular Rays, which are reflected back from the Ring-Pass-Not—must be thought of in pairs, each one being in special association with its opposite number, so that the true movement is a figure ∞, the outgoing flow being above in one half of the circle, and below in the opposite half. Herein is a very deep truth, closely related to practical occultism.

These new movements set up stresses among themselves which give rise to a series of concentric rings of movement, so that the Cosmos becomes divided up into segments of influence. The movements of the spinning Rays and the concentric Circles are known as the great 'secondaries'. There are twelve Rays and seven concentric Circles.

Within the segments are set up the movements which are known as 'Tangentials'. The nearest analogy to these is the Brownian movement of atoms, the intersecting of the Circles and Rays giving rise to angles, and the sharp tangential movement thus occasioned introduces a new factor into the Cosmos.

You now perceive that we have studied three types of movement.

(a) The interaction of the primal Rings.

(b) The interaction of the secondary Rays and Circles.

(c) The tangential movements occasioned by the opposition of the angles in the secondaries.

In these tangential movements the lines of force are continually crossing each other's paths, being confined to small segments of the Cosmos. Where they cross, a vortex is set up by the opposing influences' modifying of each others' actions. Therefore, instead of proceeding in these slight curves which give rise to enormous circles, they are deflected into a new movement and, gyrating about each other, become relatively static, thus setting up a composite unit—two forces, which no longer are influenced independently by the attractions of the greater forces, but are influenced together. Thus are atoms formed—two interlocking forces, setting up a vortex and gyrating about each other instead of circling the limits of the Cosmos.

I have described the formation of the 'prime atom'. These atoms acting as units, likewise perceive the attraction of the movements about them and begin to move in their turn, and the same process occurs again. Atoms in movement meet and gyrate, and so the process is continued. The tendency of the composite atoms is to travel towards the periphery, and of the simple atoms to remain near the centre. It is thus that the planes of Cosmic matter are developed.

To recapitulate, we have:

1. The movement of the Rings.
2. The movement of the Rays and concentric Circles.
3. The movement of the Tangentials within the segments.
4. The movement of the vortices.
5. The movement of the composite Atoms.

You will meet these numbers again.

1. refers to The Absolute.
2. refers to The Manifest.
3. refers to Evolution.
4. refers to Form.
5. refers to Life.

You have had described to you the types of movement which make up the Cosmos. The primary Rings and the secondary Rays and Circles. Now these are the basis of a Cosmos, and their influences are the underlying influences of that Cosmos. Their revolution it is which makes the great cycles—the 'Days' and 'Nights' of manifestation—a Day being the time when an aspect of the Cosmos is within what you would call the positive area of the magnetic field generated by the spinning Rings; and a Night when it is in the negative area.

By a knowledge of these Cosmic tides, the illuminated man can avail himself of their forces. Hence the power of a knowledge of the numbers of the secret calendar.

These, then are the original influences; they may be thought of as the framework of the Cosmos.

The tangential forces, within the segments of their inter-action, set up vortices; these vortices are the Primal Atoms. You may perceive that in the building of an atom the same laws are at work as enabled the Ring-Cosmos and the Ring-Chaos to build the Cosmos. It is the Law of the Opposing Forces which produces stability. The opposing forces having produced atoms, the atoms themselves become forces, because they move in their turn; and so, different types of tangential reactions occur—movements influenced by more than one attraction. So that, from the simple right-angled movement, produced by a single opposing force, vortices are described of a polyhedral type. You can see the materialized form of such reactions in the different types of crystal to which they give rise upon your plane.

So that you will get atoms the tangential path of whose component forces can be anything from a three-sided to a polyhedral figure.

# 4.

# The Building of the Atom

You must realize clearly that the primal atom consists of two opposing movements which gyrate about each other. These are simply vortices, but the vortices can move through space as a waterspout can move over the ocean, and these vortices can be induced to assume a secondary movement. It is these secondary movements which I refer to as being of an angular path.

So you will get the different types of atom from the prime atom, which is merely a spinning, to the spinning atom which moves in a triangle; the type which makes a square; the type which describes a five-sided figure, and a six-sided figure, etc.

These atoms attract each other, and can draw together and adhere to each other by means of what, metaphorically speaking, I will call the facets of their orbits. Thereby they can form alliances among themselves.

Thus different types of atoms arise in the Cosmos and begin to gather themselves together into composite bodies. Each composite body, as it increases in size, increases also its power of attraction, so that the tendency of the Cosmos is to aggregation, and the aggregates form adjustments among themselves, so that new forces arise periodically. These we shall consider in their turn.

You will perceive that we have now described, in addition to the great Ring forces of the Cosmos, the formation of an uncountable number of minute centres of stability of varying types, and the continued organization of the reactions among these centres.

You will also perceive that great phases would be gone through in the course of this evolution, for each new force that arose had to radiate out through the entire Cosmos until turned back in its course by the Ring-Pass-Not, and it would only be after it had returned whence it arose and so completed its circle, that it could become a constant influence in the Cosmos.

Within the limits of the Rays and Circles the newly-built atoms would cannon and rebound for aeons before any co-ordination would be induced among them. But as chance would govern the occurrence of two or more moving parallel to each other, where this occurred their forces would reinforce each other and draw yet more into the orbit of their activity, so that the mere rebound would give place to the ordered recurrence of influences, and therefore to definite paths. There are already worked out in the Cosmos the great lines of force which we call the Rays, and the currents of the Rays would gradually induce the great oceans of rebounding atoms to flow in their track. So that gradually the unco-ordinated forces are co-ordinated into the great tides of the Cosmos, and, though making their own tangential action, move also with the great tides.

I am now going to put before you a concept which may seem strange to you, but which is the basis of much in practical occultism. At the beginning of these teachings I said to you 'Space moved'. Whenever a movement has occurred in space, the flowing action thus set up remains. Space, when set in motion, never stops flowing, because it is frictionless. A force has been generated which remains. This force may be blended with other forces, so that for all practical purposes it ceases to be a separate unit, yet it still retains its original character, and, could you analyse the unit of which it forms a part, you would find it there intact.

Remember this point—space, set in motion, flows for ever. Thus, supposing, metaphorically speaking, you move your pen across the paper one inch, that movement would give rise to a current in space which would flow in its positive form in one aspect of the movement, and return in its negative form in its other aspect. That would remain; and whosoever could discern that movement in space, could discern the action which gave rise to it. This is the basis of memory, and this is the reason that it is easier to repeat a movement which has been performed before than to originate a movement and the more often it has been performed the easier is the repetition, because the momentum of space is cumulative and will finally avail to carry the movement in its current. You will find this explains much.

You have spread before you a Cosmos which arose out of space through movement, and which is movement and nothing else; and you have seen how the stresses of forces generated by these movements have given rise to an infinite number of vortices, built upon exactly the same principle as the Great Vortex which is the Cosmos, because the same laws hold good upon every scale of manifestation, being laws of relationship. You will then see that relationship occurs between the new centres of force thus built, and they tend to form new Cosmoi among themselves, built upon the same principles.

Dances of atoms give rise to new Rings-Cosmos, and the story begins again; these new universes, as they are called, while they have the same laws as the Cosmos before described, are also influenced by that framework of the Cosmos which was built before they began, and you will find that this law holds good throughout all manifestation.

We will recapitulate the teaching in relation to the Rays, the Circles and the Vortices.

The Rays and the Circles are part of the primary movement of the Cosmos. These, together with the Rings, remain constant in the Cosmos, and are referred to as the Cosmic Currents.

The Vortices are of another nature. The primary movements are circular. The Vortices start as straight movements, which, encountering opposition, assume a secondary circular movement.

There is, therefore, always a pair of forces concerned in the creation of the primal atom, and this fundamental duality extends into all combinations of which the atom is the base.

You will observe that whenever a particular sequence or series of units occurs in the rhythmical functioning of a movement, this series acts as the conditioning framework of whatever subsequent elaborations and combinations may be built up upon that foundation.

For instance, supposing a prime movement of an atom to be a three-sided tangential—A to B, B to C and C back to A, whatever secondary movements may arise (and remember this, that movement in a straight line is never so maintained after the original impulse dies away), conflicting forces reduce it to a modification of the primal circular, so that the atom, which in its movement originally pursued a triangular course, will finally arrive at a movement consisting of three spirals arranged in a triangle.

Each spiral movement will be executed under the conditions governing the A to B segment, then the B to C segment, then the C to A segment. Therefore, if you knew what the influences of the A to B segment were, you would know the nature of the primary movement underlying the spiral which alone appears to the superficial observer. This is a principle underlying astrology, and this is the reason why the Science of Numbers plays an important part in all practical applications of Cosmic principles.

The prime movement of an atom is a vortex—nothing else; a mere spinning round a core of motionless vacuum. The atom which has just been described is not a prime atom but an elaborate and complex structure. It is only when the prime atoms combine together that such secondary movements are set up.

Now an atom which is of a triangular structure can form unions with as many other atoms as it has facets. When each facet has become attached to an atom, the group is complete, and has attained a state of equilibrium of stress within itself. It can no longer grow by accretion but must act as a unit, and can only enter into association with other units of like type whose angles of stress are similar.

The primal atom, as I have said, is a simple vortex, and the composite atoms of different types arise according to the number of tangential angles into which the circumstances of counter-influences may draw the vortices. The vortices, be it noted, first arise in the angles where the Rays converge upon the Central Stillness. It is the close juxtaposition of forces which sets up the secondary currents. Therefore, in the sphere which surrounds the Central Stillness are to be found the primal atoms. These, however, soon take on the secondary tangential movement and thus form alliances among themselves by accretion, as before described.

As you have already been told, in addition to the movement of the Rays, there is the movement of the Circles about the Central Stillness. This movement gives rise to centrifugal action, and the atoms tend to swing out towards the periphery. The more complex the atom, the more strongly will it feel the centrifugal action, so that you will find that the Circles contain atoms of gradually increasing complexity as they succeed one another. These atoms, arising in the angles of the Rays, when they feel the influence of the centrifugal force, go out along the line of a Ray. Each atom, then, has in itself forces of two Rays which set up the primal vortex, and then goes out along the path of one of these Rays.

5.

# Atomic Evolution upon the Cosmic Planes

Evolution upon the Cosmic planes may first be observed as the gradual filling of the circle of space with atoms: immensely long aeons passing in the process.

Thus the prime atoms occupy Circle One. The first form of composites—Circle Two. Combinations of these composites—Circle Three, and so on.

These types of matter, as we may now call them, are thus spread in concentric spheres throughout the Cosmos, out to the limit of the Ring-Pass-Not, going out along the lines of the Rays, so that, while the first circle contains only atoms of its own type, each succeeding circle has in its atoms inter-atomic movements representative of each of the inner circles, the construction of the outermost atoms being very elaborate.

When the atoms reach the outermost sphere, a fresh force sets in; they have encountered the opposition of the Ring-Pass-Not. The atoms in the outermost circle are an exceedingly complex system of movements within movements. Having gone out from the Central Stillness with a centrifugal force, they are now rebuffed by the Ring-Pass-Not and, owing to the rebuff, return with a spiral movement. This it is which gives their peculiar formation to the Rays.

Having reached the centre, these atoms then speed outwards with a straight centrifugal motion along the line of the opposite Ray to the one by which they entered the centre, to return again in the same way, but at a slightly different angle, which will cause them, upon the next outgoing path, to follow the next Ray to the preceding one, and so work their way round the circle. When repulsed by the Ring-Pass-Not they make a circular movement upon the plane of the outermost circle, thus feeling its force from all angles. They repeat this movement upon each plane as they return.

Now, as you have already been told, each movement in space continues as a movement, therefore every influence that plays upon these atoms is registered in the reaction of stresses within their structure, so that each atom returns to the Central Stillness infinitely more complex after each journey; each Ray intersecting the circles at a different angle causes the atom travelling upon its path to experience different influences on its journey; therefore, the final complexity of these atoms, when the complete circuit has been described, though it is capable of mathematical expression cannot be conveyed to the finite intellect; but could you grasp the geometry of these atoms, could you know their numerical calculus you would hold the key to the explanation of the Universe.

These structures are still referred to as atoms—not as in the case of chemistry on the hypothesis that they cannot be resolved into any simpler structure, being homogeneous—but on the basis that, though composite, when once formed they cannot be resolved but are permanently units.

It will thus be seen that the flowing out of the atoms to the circumference and their return to the centre marks a phase of evolution of the Cosmos; and the completion of the circuit of the Rays by an atom marks a phase of evolution of that atom. When it has completed this circuit, it has experienced all the forces that the Cosmos can offer it, and when all the atoms evolved have completed the circuit (and the evolution of atoms upon such a tide is limited, because after a certain proportion of force has taken up a tangential form, a state of equilibrium is reached within the Cosmos, for evolution proceeds from the first movement of a state of uncompensated force until equilibrium is reached) this is the completion of an evolution—a state of equilibrium, and therefore a relative stillness.

You will observe that we have now described three phases of Cosmic evolution. The development of the Rings was the first phase. They gave rise to each other and acted and reacted on each other till a state of equilibrium was reached. Then, though they were static in relation to each other, that is to say, though in constant movement within themselves they maintained their relationship constant towards each other and must continue ever so to do since there is nothing to disturb them, the vortices set up by the movements of the Rings gave rise to secondary movements—the Rays and Circles. These, starting upon their respective courses, developed them until they also became static in relation to each other, and a second phase of evolution was passed through. Thirdly these in their turn, gave rise to the tangential movements which built the atoms.

It will thus be seen that a phase of development is succeeded by a phase of equilibrium during which that which has been developed is maintained, but nothing becomes, its status is unchanged. These phases may be known to you under the names of the 'Days' and 'Nights of God'—the Day of evolution—the Night of static balance, and then the overcoming of one set of forces by another, which causes the balance slowly to dip into manifestation again.

The equilibrium is then over and new forces are set going. These forces are based upon the relationship of the units previously built up, and are influenced by the prime determinants—the Rings, the Rays, and the Circles. Within these limits, and subject to the nature of the units upon which they act, they may form fresh combinations, permutations, and rhythms of action and reaction, until the new forces have found their equilibrium; and in their utmost completion and development, when the final combination has been achieved, then again become static in the Cosmic balance until such period as the balance shall again be overset.

The oversetting of the balance is due to the same forces as set up the primal Rings—the fact that movement generates movement and sets up a sphere of swirl outside its own path. That is why, though every fresh set of forces set in movement must attain to a final equilibrium, being only a maintaining of position of movements relative one to another, being therefore a 'relative' stillness, must always overbalance and fly out into a new phase of evolution, because this is a Cosmos built of movement, and movement generates movement.

You have got, I think, a clear concept of what has been called the framework of the Cosmos—the Rings, the Rays and the Circles. These, having long since completed their evolution, have settled down to a static condition, the only change which occurs being that of the Cosmos passing through the positive and negative spheres of influence, four to the cycle. These make great phases—the phase when the constructive influence is intensified, and the phase when the destructive influence is intensified. The Circles and the Rays flow steadily in their orbits, but when the positive phase is in being, the outgoing currents are speeded up, and when the negative phase is in being the incoming currents are speeded up.

The great Rings—three in number—are the Primal Trinity, known to you as the 'Absolute', though the implication of the word Absolute is known to few, that is to say, the term Absolute has been used in teaching pupils without the pupils realizing its full import. Because there are three Rings the 'Absolute' is a Triune Force. These three, operating together with an indissoluble interaction, are the Three which are One, and the

One which is Three. Refer the terms of the Athanasian Creed to this Trinity and you will grasp the meaning of the Initiate who dictated it.

The Rays form together a complex system which will be referred to under the name Zodiac.

The Circles are the Cosmic Planes.

The Central Sun is that point in space which would be reached if a line from the sun of your system were drawn to the star known as 'Alpha Centauri' and thence projected.

You have seen how the atoms arise—as vortices in the angles of the Rays; how, in their simple form, they remain upon the first of the Cosmic Planes wherein they originated. When, however, they form alliances among themselves and become composite, their weight, metaphorically speaking, that is to say their susceptibility to influences, is increased, and susceptibility to influence is all that weight is esoterically. That fact forms the basis of limitation and flight through space. Cut off your susceptibility to influence and you can move freely.

When the atoms become composite, centrifugal forces drive them outwards and, finding the paths of the flowing Rays, they proceed by these as being the lines of least resistance. When they reach the next circle they remain there, having found their level of gravity. Then presently some composite atoms form additional associations and are again swung out by the path of a Ray. Therefore, you will see that it is only when the extremely elaborate atoms of the Seventh Circle form alliances that they start back up the spiral to the Central Sun.

# 6.

# The Beginnings of a Solar System

You have heard how these atoms in their journeying progress up and down the Rays, for they are too highly evolved, too composite to be allowed to remain upon any plane. When an atom, however, has completed the circuit of the Rays and seeks to start out again, it finds its place taken by atoms of later development. It cannot enter that stream for it is full; it must therefore remain in the Central Stillness. No atom goes twice round the circuit, and those atoms which have come home rest from their pilgrimage; and when the last atom has come home the whole creation sinks to sleep, and the Cosmic Tides set inwards as the Ring-Cosmos swings to its negative phase.

Meanwhile, the Rays flow and return and the Circles spin on their path, but the atoms stir not, though each within itself contains an infinitude of balanced movement. When, however, the Ring-Cosmos passes into a new phase, fresh attractions pull towards the periphery.

Now the influence of the Ring-Cosmos and the Ring-Chaos must be clearly understood. When the influence of the Ring-Chaos predominates, there is an unbalancing force, that is to say, the Ring-Chaos is in its positive phase; and when the influence of the Ring-Cosmos predominates, there is a compensating force, it atones for the excessive force of Chaos.

Thus, Chaos calls outwards into space, and Cosmos balances and compensates until a static condition is produced.

We have seen that the first phase of atomic evolution has concluded with all the atoms evolved to their utmost complexity, withdrawn from the outer circles and clustered around the Central Sun. The Ring-Cosmos has done its work. All is balanced, static and sleeps, but as the cycle revolves, the Ring-Chaos has its turn and it oversets the balance which has been achieved, and the most composite of the atoms feel first the centrifugal forces urging them, and yet again seek to come forth; so the great units come out once more down the lines of the Rays, but they proceed now not through empty space, for each Circle is populated by atoms of a different degree of complexity, whose specific gravity holds them at that distance from the Central Stillness.

These composite organisms, finding themselves thus surrounded by simpler organisms, draw them about themselves by the force of their whirling revolution, and thus, as they progress outward, each becomes surrounded by a sphere of the matter of each plane which it carries with it.

Now the Great Organisms which come forth are built up around the prime atoms of different tangential angles, and these, according to their numerical compositions, differ in size and also weight, and therefore find their appropriate bourne on different planes or Circles where they are held by their relative specific gravity. The Ray can carry them no further.

The first phase of atomic evolution was essentially concerned with the Rays, but in the second going forth of the Great Organisms, the Circles have their places, and these Great Organisms go not out and back, but revolve with the circles, each in its appointed track.

Therefore, evolution has now built up, in addition to the primal statics—the Rings, the Rays and the Circles—two more sets of statics—the atoms, each in its plane according to type that, owing to their nature, have settled down having found their specific position, and the Great Organisms, which have also settled down, each to its radius of movement. The atoms move tangentially among themselves, and the Great Organisms revolve around the Central Sun, passing through the influences of the Rays as they revolve, and therefore, are relatively static, subject only to the cyclic changes produced by the phases of the Rings, and the influences of the Rays as they pass through them.

Each of the Great Organisms can attract to itself as much of the matter of each plane that it passes through on its way out at the beginning of this second phase of its evolution as it can hold by the attraction of its mass, and it can pass out as far as the momentum of its mass can take it from the Central Sun; therefore, its position is determined by the angles of the facets of the primal atom upon which it is built. That is to say, if the vortex set up in the angles of the Rays moved in a three-sided path, it could go no further than the first plane beyond the Central Stillness; it would have to be a ten-sided figure to reach the seventh plane and evolve there.* You will thus see that each of these Great organisms has for its key the number of the angles in the path of the original vortex which gives rise to it. This forms its limit and determines the

* See end of Chapter 5.

circumference of its influence. This it is which determines its particular Ring-Pass-Not.

We have, therefore, developed a number of Great Organisms which, being exposed to the influence of the Rings, the Rays, and the Circles, themselves develop upon similar lines. That is to say, each of these aggregates of atoms sorts itself out according to the nature of the atoms composing it, and these atoms, having developed under their prime influences, and having those influences established in their natures by the action and interaction they set up, form miniatures of the Great Cosmos, and those Great Organisms, those, that is to say, which are of the seventh plane, are known unto you as Solar Systems.

That, in brief outline, is the history of the genesis of a Solar System, of Solar Systems in general—of your own in particular.

There are many other Solar Systems upon the seventh plane besides your own. Some of them are known to you as the stars, but the few you know are but an infinitesimal fraction of those even of your own plane which you do not know; and there are systems upon other planes which are not perceptible to you in your present phase of evolution. You will perceive that each phase of evolution gives rise to a grand unity, though a complex one.

First the system of the Rings, which is the 'Absolute'.

Then the system of the Rays and Circles which is the Cosmos.

Then the Great Organisms which we will call the Universes, also according to their planes.

You have then the numerical series. If you will number them, you will see how the numbers run. The Universes or Solar Systems are of the fourth Cosmic phase of evolution.

Now these Universes undergo internal evolution upon the same lines as the Cosmos, and these phases of internal evolution continue until they also become static within themselves and their composite atoms flow into the Central Sun, each of its own system, and rest there.

Then once again the influences of the Ring-Chaos break up the Cosmic balances, the Great Organisms, developed in each solar system, go forth and bursting through the Ring-Pass-Not of that solar system, circle about it as satellites. Whereupon, the solar system which underwent disintegration starts once again a new phase of its evolution whose units are the composite atoms evolved in its previous evolution; passes again through all the phases of evolution, and again flings off the 'star seed'.

Meanwhile, those Great Organisms which are first scattered, are repeating the process, each in its turn, so that the solar systems become in their turn Cosmoi to those Great Organisms to which they gave birth, and so this process, which I will call 'The Stellar Evolution', goes on till a static condition is reached among the Great Organisms and their progeny, and then, the influence of the Ring-Pass-Not coming into action, a great system is sent back to the Central Stillness to come forth again when the influences of the Ring-Chaos call it out; and such process continues until such time as the organization of the Cosmos becomes so mighty in the force it has generated, that it bursts the Ring-Pass-Not, and the Great Organisms rush forth into the unmanifest, and by their swirling movement gather 'space' about them and, in their turn, build new 'Cosmoi'. Such is the story of Cosmic evolution.

You will perceive that each phase of evolution begets an organized system of forces. These forces react to all influences that play upon them, and they register the reaction in the movements of the space that is under their influence. They are therefore sentient, because they react and register through experience. So that even the three Primal Rings are sentient and capable of development, but they are so vast, these Rings, and so simple (because the influences that act upon them are so few) that the Individuality, though it exceeds the span of all imagination, is exceedingly primitive. Yet it is upon this vast and simple type that your Individuality is built up. Therefore it is that you—small as you are—have your affinities with those Cosmic Beings and are influenced by their phases, from the 'Absolute' down to the atom of your own Earth. This it is which in essence is the Secret Wisdom. For the uninitiated man is acted upon by these forces, but the Initiate, by his knowledge, transcends their influence, and uses them for his own ends. Should his ends be those of the Cosmic evolution, he grows and develops through all its phases till he attains that static condition which is completeness and, following the laws of the Great Organisms of which he is now one, he gives rise himself to a system.

7.

# The Evolution of a Solar System

You have duly received the first part of the work. Your minds need to be thoroughly imbued with the principles previously mentioned in order that you may understand what is to follow.

I will briefly recapitulate. Motion in space is the Prime. When its circuit is concluded it forms the Ring-Cosmos, which gives rise to the Ring-Chaos, which, by its secondary influence, causes the Ring-Cosmos to form the Ring-Pass-Not. This is the Three or Trinity.

The inflowing influences, converging upon the centre and radiating to the periphery, are the Rays—the Twelve.

The motions of the Cosmos give rise to the Seven—the Circles or planes.

The converging angles of the Rays give rise to the tangential motions.

These, when in opposition, give rise to the Prime Atoms.

The atoms, moving in their turn along the paths of differing angularity, form the complex atoms which centrifugal force sorts out upon their planes.

These finally, in the outermost plane when they combine again, not being able to go any further return to the centre. These are called the 'journeying' atoms. The others are the static atoms, because they have settled down.

So that you have in the Central Stillness no atoms, but only the Primal Cosmic Forces.

Upon the first plane you have atoms whose path is a triangular one; therefore, the Number upon this plane is based upon three; at first the simplest atom presents three aspects, and the most complex is a composite of three. The atoms of the second plane have four for their Number, and the third plane have five; the fourth plane six, and so on, down to the seventh plane which has nine. These are referred to as Secondary Numbers, whereas the Numbers of the Cosmic Forces are the Primary Numbers. You have, then, as Primaries—one, three, seven, and twelve; and as Secondaries—three to nine inclusive.

The Prime Tertiary is ten. Ten is the Number of evolution, because it is the atoms of ten angles that evolve.

You will perceive from the foregoing that the Primaries gave rise to each other, and have settled down into stability, cycle following cycle in orderly progression. They have completed their course, and have achieved the maximum complexity of which they are capable. Under the influence of the changing phases of the Primaries the secondary movements pursue their courses.

The secondary movements obey the laws of their own natures, subject to the laws and conditions of the Primaries.

Likewise, with the tertiaries each plane of existence pursues its course, subject to the influences of that phase which gave rise to it.

For example, the Ring-Cosmos passes through its positive and negative phases. The Rays therefore are sometimes flowing faster upon the negative and outgoing arc when the negative phase of the Ring-Cosmos is prevailing upon their segment; and sometimes the inflowing or positive aspect is speeded up, as their segment of the universe is covered by the positive phase.

Each segment of a Ray is influenced by the circle in whose area it lies. Therefore it will be seen that a journeying atom will be subject, at a given moment, to the influence of the Ray upon which it is travelling; to its position upon that Ray, whether upon the outflowing or inflowing aspect; to the plane through which it is passing; and to the phases of the Ring-Cosmos. Therefore, if you wish to understand the conditions of a given travelling atom, it is not enough to know the facets of its path, you must also know the phases of the influences to which its nature is reacting. This is called 'Sidereal Astrology', but the phases of this astrology are so vast that they concern only the lives of the Solar Systems, just as the planetary astrology concerns the phases of the planets. The nearest point of contact which you have to Sidereal Astrology is known to you as the Zodiac. It is obvious, then, if you consider the life of a man, you must consider it in relation to the solar system of which he forms a part, and you must also consider that solar system in relation to the Cosmos. Sidereal Astrology will give you the phases of evolution.

You see, then, that there are atoms of specific types that have settled down permanently upon each plane, and move at constant distances from the Central Stillness in the same way that a liquid, containing different substances in solution, will, if placed in a glass tube which is swirled rapidly round at the end of a string, show clearly the sorting out of the component parts of the mixture according to their specific gravity, the heaviest, or most composite, towards the periphery, so that at the conclusion of the process you can perceive the graduated bands of different types of substance. These atoms have proceeded as far as their essential nature permits them to proceed in evolution. You will perceive that each new phase of evolution achieves the utmost complexity that its factors permit, and then settles down to a rhythmic repetition of the sequence it has reached.

The fresh phase of evolution, which begins when the next phase of the Ring-Chaos overtopples the stability achieved, starts where the last phase finished, because it already has in its nature all that the last phase achieved. You see now the significance of the maxim 'As above, so below, but after another manner.' The Cosmos is the framework upon which all is built; you start where God leaves off; therefore, what is in God is in you, and something of your own which is called 'free will', though it is an unsuitable name.

Now, with regard to the evolution of the travelling atoms, these give rise to Solar Systems.

You will remember in the previous lectures that these solar systems arose on different planes of the universe according to their Cosmic specific gravity. That is to say, they start their evolution at different phases of Cosmic development. But you will remember that the outgoing atoms gather up matter from each plane they pass through, to build into their universe.

With those systems which are developed upon other planes than yours I will not deal in detail in the present course of study for they are too remote for our immediate purposes.

I will consider, however, the phases of development through which pass systems that originate upon the seventh Cosmic plane, of which your solar system is an example. Let us therefore trace the life of a particular travelling atom which is to become your sun and attendant system of planets.

You will remember that it has been round the circuit of the Cosmic Rays and experienced their twelve influences, both positive and negative and that it has in its composition matter of the seven Cosmic planes. Its Numbers, therefore, are:

Three because it is under the influence of the three Rings.
Seven because it has matter of seven types.
Twelve because it has been acted upon by the Twelve Rays; and each

of the seven planes of matter will have its particular Number, from three to nine inclusive.

This atom, having passed out through the placid planes of Cosmic matter and taking with it as much as it can draw from each plane arrives finally at its own plane where an equilibrium is established between the centrifugal and centripetal forces of the Cosmos and its own bulk. It then settles down upon its orbit.

The Cosmic influences to which it is exposed can be calculated in an orderly sequence, because they are definitely established. It will pass round the twelve Rays, and experience the changes of the phases of the Rings; and, in addition to this, the influences of the Great Organisms of the other planes will, whenever their orbits happen to bring them near each other (for they move at different paces upon different planes), influence the matter drawn from that plane in the make-up of that system. That is an important point.

(You can see that there are times when the Lower Astral would receive a stimulus and times when the Upper Spiritual would likewise, although this is not so strong as the corresponding Cosmic plane is not so near. This is one of the things that check evolution and often set up trouble in a system.)

This Great Organism that we are considering has settled down to its orbit, and you can conceive of it as a nucleus of the original travelling atom surrounded by great cloudy, unformed, unorganized belts of matter of the different planes. These are held about it by the attraction of its mass; and the limit and extent of its attraction marks the extent of the system. Like all else in the Cosmos, this mass has a rotating movement which is derived from the original central atom.

The movement of that atom within its orbit gradually, in the course of untold ages, connects its movement with the whole, and the mass flattens out into a spinning disc; then the motions, which you saw in the formation of a Cosmos, are gone through, because the laws of motion are the same upon every plane, and the solar system sorts out its matter into seven planes owing to specific gravity.

# 8.

# The Evolution of a Great Entity

Conceive now the experience of existence as it is apprehended by the dawning consciousness of a Great Entity.

Hitherto we have looked at the evolution of points of manifestation from without; we will now consider the matter from within, as it appears subjectively to that Cosmic unit of manifestation referred to as a Great Entity.

First, conceive the sensation of a whirling and no other sensation at all. Conceive yourself becoming so habituated to that whirling that its cessation would occasion a sensation, but not its continuance.

Conceive a secondary motion developing, perceived at first because of its newness, and losing its stimulative power owing to habituation, as did the primary, and so on in sequence.

You will now perceive that movements that are habitual must be maintained if an absence of distracting sensation, which is the basis of attention, is to be arrived at. Therefore, the accustomed movements are implicit in the 'being' of that which is based upon them, and, when awakening into manifestation, it will always seek to establish those motions as the basis of its existence.

Now, recall the phases of movement to which the Great Entities became habituated in the course of Cosmic evolution which led to their development, and you will see that all those movements have become implicit in their nature and will be reproduced when they, in turn, set out upon that *inner* elaboration which constitutes the next phase of Cosmic evolution—the phase of the evolution of the Great Entities; bearing in mind that upon whatever plane or Ring of the Cosmos the Entities settle down for a cycle of evolution, the numerical values of the evolution will be determined thereby.

We will now consider the evolution of the Great Entity with which we are especially concerned.

Implicit in its nature are the phases of the Cosmos, hence the significance of the maxim—'As above, so below, but after another manner'. Whatever is developed under a certain set of conditions reproduces those conditions in the recapitulation through which it goes prior to the undertaking of original development.

The Great Entity, then, having this basis of cosmically evolved factors to work upon, combines and re-combines them into the infinite diversity of a manifested universe. Therefore, the infinite diversity of a manifested universe can be resolved into the prime simplicity of the Cosmic beginnings. Each phase or aspect of the universe has its origin in a similar phase or aspect of the Cosmos.

A Great Entity, having settled down upon its Cosmic orbit, proceeds upon its work of evolution. Having had the Cosmic factors implanted in its nature by its experiences, it proceeds independently of the Cosmic impulse to bring them into function of its own momentum, which momentum may be termed 'a Cosmic Will'.

You will perceive that we are still speaking in terms of dynamics. It is not until a high degree of evolution has been achieved that we can speak in terms of psychology, but there is an unbroken line of development from movement to thought. Tangential movement is a simple form of reaction. Thought is an infinitely complex form of reaction. It is a question of difference of degree, not of difference of kind. Fundamentally, there is no difference of kind in anything, because all can be reduced to the prime Central Stillness. Upon the planes of manifestation, however, there are differences of kind, because the Rays issuing from the Central Stillness diverge as they proceed. As consciousness is limited in its objective functioning to one plane at a time, a unity of the innermost cannot be perceived save by the consciousness that stands therein; and, the transition from one plane to another of any Ray or line of force being marked by a sub-division of that Ray, you will perceive that there are differences of kind in manifestation, although there is a fundamental unity. Differences of degree are reckoned along the length of the same Ray; differences of kind are reckoned in the sequence of Rays round the circle. (This digression which, strictly speaking, belongs to another section of this subject, is made here to ensure clearness of comprehension in the argument pursued.)

A Great Entity commences its evolution by developing not the Cosmic Rings, but the *concepts* of those Rings. That is to say, it puts in motion the memories of the experiences it underwent when that which afterwards condensed into its substance was part of the primordial swirlings. It knows 'good' and 'evil' and therefore is a God. It is the knowledge of good and evil which enables it to manifest, because the 'good' is a dynamism, and the 'evil' is a thrust-block. The Ring-Pass-Not of a universe is the limitation of the attention of the Great Entity forming that universe. It is its determination to concentrate its attention upon the task it has set itself.

A travelling atom, having passed through all the phases of Cosmic evolution up to that of which its production is the crown and completion, makes a final journey to the Central Stillness. Then, by the overbalancing of the equipoise, it issues forth, but with this difference—it has itself become owing to its development a centre of attraction. Thereby it draws to itself a certain number of the atoms of each plane through which it passes until it arrives at the Cosmic belt which is decreed as its habitation by its own specific gravity in relation to the centrifugal forces of the Cosmic swirlings. There will be, then, in this new organization thus formed, a central nucleus consisting of the travelling atom. This central nucleus will have implicit in it the modes of reaction to which it became habituated during its experience of the phases of Cosmic evolution.

In order to achieve the absence of sensation to which the presence and continuance of habituated reactions in their accustomed ordered sequence alone can give rise, this nuclear atom continues to make its accustomed reactions owing to the momentum of its particles. These actions upon its part induce the corresponding reactions of the loose aggregations of matter from each Cosmic plane that are gathered about it. Thus is built up a miniature Cosmos.

As may be perceived by a little thought, this miniature Cosmos with the nuclear atom corresponding to the Central Stillness which, in the larger Cosmos, transmuted all reactions into actions, has the same function performed by the nuclear atom. At the same time, the entire organism is subject to the phases of the Cosmic forces—its synthetic aspect receiving an impulse during the phases of the 'Cosmic Day', those segments of the circle in which the positive or stimulative forces are predominant; and its analytical aspect receiving a stimulus when passing through those segments of the circle in which the negative forces predominate. Likewise, as it passes through the sphere of influence of each Ray, will the corresponding forces in its own nature receive an additional stimulus.

You may conceive, then, this Great Organism travelling round a circle which is divided into four quarters—positive and negative alternately—and in addition to this each quarter is subdivided into the spheres of influence of three Rays. You have now the keys to the so-called 'Days' and 'Nights of God' and to the periods of evolution; but, as this Great Organism we are considering is itself a miniature Cosmos, you will perceive that a more speedy cycle will be performed within its own nature.

In addition to these influences there is another set of influences to be considered. These are the gravitational attractions of other Great Organisms upon other planes of the Cosmos.

The relations between one Great Organism and others upon its own plane are fixed and determined before further evolution begins, and, being constant, need not be considered. But the revolutions of Great Entities upon other planes of the Cosmos are conducted at different paces, and without relation to Entities of other planes than their own. Therefore, they will pass in line with each other periodically, momentarily blocking the pull of the central attraction upon those organisms further out than themselves, and also exerting a gravitational attraction upon all particles of their own plane and planes above their own in the mass of a Great Organism on an outer path.

This cutting off temporarily of the central attraction upsets the equilibrium of the outer Organism, removing the centripetal check upon the centrifugal force, but the tendency of certain types of molecules to fly inward towards the attracting body tends to counterbalance this. Also the whole *will* of the nuclear atom of that Organism is to maintain constant the habituated conditions which have become the law of its nature. The habituated conditions, it may be said in parenthesis, are among those sequences which man names 'Natural Laws' when he discovers them.

Likewise, the forces of the Cosmos tend to maintain equilibrium, compensating each other. But there occur, nevertheless, at irregular intervals, conditions which require compensation, and these give rise to varying degrees of irregularity in the movement of Great Entities, and hence to the presence of 'positive evil', sin, and disease within their spheres.

The Cosmos itself has to strive for adjustment at the commencement of each phase of its evolution, and the irregularities which occur before adjustment is effected and which have to be pulled straight in the course of evolution are the origin of evil in the sense in which the word is used popularly.

'Cosmic evil' is a limitation—an opposition, and is the prime condition of manifestation; it is what we have called 'negative evil'.

This Cosmic evil, the 'Divine evil', the 'Divine death', is implicit in each Great Entity, and is the basis of its manifestation and evolution. For without limitation—finiteness—there can be no manifestation, and without death or the discarding of the outworn, there can be no progress.

These elements, then, of Cosmic opposition are always present in a manifested universe; but the universal evil, under its two aspects of sin or perverted force and disease or perverted form, are due to the irregularities of orbit caused by the passings of Great Organisms upon different planes of the Cosmos. These are always found in their extreme form at the beginning of an evolution and are gradually adjusted in the course of an evolution as compensations are made, until, at the end of an evolution, a perfect and rhythmical balance of the whole Cosmos has been achieved—a synthesis of action and reaction which maintains stability.

# 9.
# The Creation of a Universe

> And the earth was without form and void, and darkness was upon the face of the deep.

We have now, you will perceive, traced two sets of phases of evolution—the Cosmic phases, and the more rapid recapitulation of the phases in the development of a Great Entity. And we have studied that Great Entity in its relation to the Cosmos which is its environment, and to the Central Stillness which is the compensation of all the forces of the Cosmos and which is its God. We will now consider the life of a Great Entity in relation to the universe of which it is itself the God—the Creator—the Conditioner—and the Sustainer.

You will perceive that a Great Entity comes out from the Central Stillness and takes its place upon its appointed circuit, and constructs its organism under the influence of the negative or destructive phase of the Cosmos. This may seem strange to you, that creation should take place under the influence of a destructive force of the Cosmos, or of any other organization which, by overbalancing the synthesis of forces achieved in a phase of evolution, causes them to embark upon a fresh phase of development in order to re-establish their harmony. And as they commence this phase with the experience of the preceding phase implicit in their nature, they commence where the last phase ended; they 'climb upon its shoulders', and thereby evolution rises to a great complexity, for it has now become an organization of organisms. You will see this principle prevailing throughout all things, great and little, above and below; it is one of the Cosmic principles, and one little known, if known at all.

Likewise, the phases of development during which a Great Entity organizes itself are internal and therefore subjective. They are not carried out under the stimulus of sensations derived from external conditions, but under the stimulus of feelings arising from internal conditions and the phases correspond to the phases of existence which a human soul passes through between death and birth. These phases having been completed, a Great Entity has arrived at the greatest degree of organization of which it is capable with the conditions at its disposal and can go no further. It being organized throughout, each part is affected by and responds to changes in any other part. It is therefore fully conscious, for consciousness is but awareness, and awareness is but reaction to a stimulus. The conditions of its nature, being habitual in their sequence, no longer give rise to conscious stimuli. The Great Entity has, therefore, a consciousness, but nothing of which it can be conscious except itself. The Cosmos, be it noted, being entirely habitual to this Entity, forms the conditioning background of its consciousness, which is comparable to the human subconsciousness of the automatic level.

It has, then, by the sensations of its own nature, a concept of itself, of which it is aware. Here, then, is a novel sensation, and it dwells upon it. This is the self-consciousness of a Great Entity. This is creation–'And God made man in His own image and likeness'. A universe is a concept in the mind of a Great Entity. It is created by the self-contemplation of a Great Entity.

The consciousness of the Great Entity, being aware of this image of itself as a whole, next becomes aware of the changes in the proportions of the forces of its own nature caused by the Cosmic influences through which it has passed, thus giving rise to fresh concepts concerning itself, and these concepts are added to the existing concepts, conditioning it historically. These are different outflowings of creative force concerning which you have heard.

This teaching concerning the subjective and objective aspects of a Great Entity is the key to the doctrine of pantheism, which as generally understood is a half-truth. For a Great Organism holds in its memory the Cosmic conditions, although it, itself, does not contain the Cosmos, of which it is a part. Likewise, the mental picture of itself projected by a Great Entity reflects that Great Entity in its entirety, being the product of perfected consciousness, but it is not that Entity of which it is the emanation, though it is entirely conditioned by the nature and experiences of that Entity, having no other origin, and being exposed to no other influences whatsoever, for it has no other existence save in the consciousness of the Entity conceiving it, therefore it is not directly affected by Cosmic conditions, being of another order of creation than the Great Entities which are the fellows of its creator, and each of which, in course of time, projects its concept of itself. It is, however, indirectly affected by the Cosmic phases, because the Great Entity which is the basis of its existence is affected by them. It is this fact that secures a universe from disturbance and permits of no intervening influence intruding in the relations between it and its Creator and Sustainer—its God.

Its God, therefore, is omnipotent as far as it is concerned, though Himself conditioned by the conditions of the Cosmos.

Its God is infinite as far as it is concerned, because He is 'all that is' to it. What He is not, *is not*, as far as it is concerned. But He himself is finite in relation to the Cosmos, which is infinite as far as He is concerned, being 'all that is' for Him, though itself finite in relation to the Unmanifest.

'Omnipotence' here means freedom from the influence of any conditioning power: and 'Infinity' means the sum total of the influences to which an organism is capable of reacting. A universe, then, is a thought-form projected by the mind of God, Who to it is omnipotent and infinite.

As we have already seen, a Great Entity projects its concept of itself. This, however, is not the beginning of objectivization in a universe, though dealt with first in the order of instruction in order to make that which follows more comprehensible; for the Great Entity, when it projected the image of itself, gained substance of the same nature as the projection, awaiting the organization which that projection should bring about.

It will be recalled that the Great Entity gathered about itself atoms of each Cosmic plane, out of which it formed its body. These atoms themselves are entities, though of a lesser degree of development than the Great Entity of which they form a part. Being of lesser development, the full recapitulatory growth is achieved earlier. Each atom, having realized itself, has created a concept of itself. These concepts, projected by the atoms, are not atoms, but so many units of knowledge of ways in which reaction is possible. They are not, therefore, sorted out into concentric belts, because there is nothing in them upon which gravitation can act. They are merely forms of reaction.

Now, the consciousness of a Great Entity is not aware of the individual reactions of its atoms, any more than the consciousness of man is aware of the individual consciousness of the cells composing his body. Therefore, when it seeks to conceive an image of itself, it has to take the reactions of the different types of atoms in their respective aggregates, and is dependent upon the atomic concepts for the creation of the necessary atomic images. Therefore, the Great Entity has to create its concept of itself in objective substance, and is therefore limited and bound by conditions of the nature of the already created images which it utilizes.

Thus, the atoms, by conceiving their own images, perform the primal act of creation.

The first act of creation proceeds from the *body* of God, and is but a mass of unorganized units—'Darkness was upon the face of the deep.' These units, having no organization and consequently no relationship among themselves, could not attain to objective consciousness, but the concept of the Great Entity, based upon its Cosmic experiences, as soon as it became projected organized them into relationships, and they then became conscious of each other, and became affected by each other.

It will thus be seen that the Cosmic atoms created the atoms of each prime sub-plane of a plane of manifestation, and that the atoms thus created, by being brought into relationship each with its own kind by action of the Great Entity, developed the sub-planes.

The prime sub-plane of each plane, then, has a direct relationship with its corresponding plane of Cosmic substance, and consequently is influenced by the Great Entities upon that plane. Hence there is always a certain opposition to the Great Entity of a universe on the part of the atoms which form its matter. This is a very important point.

We have then, first, the projection of the atomic concepts. Then later, the projection of the Great Entity's concept of itself, which organizes those atoms into a miniature Cosmos, which is called a universe in these papers, to distinguish it from that stage of existence which gave rise to its parent and Creator.

# 10.

# The Beginnings of Consciousness

And the Spirit of God moved upon the face of the waters,
and God said 'Let there be Light', and there was Light.

You have heard in previous lectures how the atoms, or units of manifestation of a universe, are formed, and also how the currents and tides of Divine Power are set flowing through them, so that an exact replica of the Cosmos is formed in miniature—the correspondences being exact, save that the cycles of a universe, moving in a smaller radius, have a more rapid rhythm. (Note that a rhythm is but a sequence of repetitions.)

Two phases of Logoidal evolution have been outlined:

(a) The phase of the development of the matter of a universe.

(b) The phase of the development of the Tides and Rays.

The one is the raw material out of which a universe is made. The other is the skeleton—the framework—upon which it is built.

We have, then, enormous quantities of atoms differentiated only into planes and sub-planes of planes. Seven distinct types and seven sub-types of each type.

We will now consider the third phase of Logoidal evolution.

At the beginning of an evolution, the Logos is alone in that sphere which is afterwards to become Its universe. It is conscious only of Itself, for there is no object in existence within that sphere of which It can be conscious.

It will thus be seen that the Logos reverses the order of the psychologist's concept of the evolution of consciousness, having first Cosmic consciousness, then self-consciousness, and then objective consciousness.

The Logos, then, is now aware that a thought-form has been projected from Its consciousness into Its aura. For under one aspect the universe may be conceived of as the aura of God.

This consciousness of an object produces a reaction in the Logoidal consciousness. There is a subject-object adaptation, and this adaptation produces a corresponding modification in the reflected universe, which becomes capable of an object-subject reaction. Thus a relationship, or reciprocity, is established between the Logos, or Great Entity, and that projected image of the Logoidal consciousness which is the incipient universe.

It must not be thought, however, that the Logoidal consciousness is limited to awareness of Its objectified universe. The Logoidal focussed consciousness, or conscious consciousness, is thus limited, for a focussed or conscious consciousness can only be built up out of awareness of and reactions to objects; but the Logoidal sub-consciousness is aware of the Cosmos, and the consciousness is influenced by the sub-consciousness which is its basis and background; and as the Cosmic Tides ebb, flow, and move round the circle, the corresponding aspects of the Logoidal sub-consciousness are stimulated by their influences, and the sensations thus engendered in the Logoidal consciousness are forthwith incorporated in the self-projection, which is the universe, and the conscious consciousness of the Logos perceives them there, so that an infinite series of reactions and modifications of reactions proceeds, at first in broad and simple movements but gradually multiplying into an inconceivable complexity.

All these modifications influence the atomic matter of the incipient universe and determine the nature and characteristics of its components. It is these characterizations that are subsequently discovered by man as Natural Laws, or observed sequences. Thus are the natures of things determined, they are built into them by the Logoidal reactions to the condition of its Cosmic environment, and these modifications are constantly proceeding. They do not endure for a phase and cease, but continue as long as the atomic sub-planes to which they correspond are in existence. Thus an elemental evolution proceeds apart from the evolution of Life and Form as we know it.

You have perceived in the course of these lectures that each phase of evolution, whether Cosmic or Logoidal, starts with a new type of action and reaction, and every possibility of new reactions to reactions already established. The scheme resembles the possible number of changes that can be rung upon a chime of bells, and the addition of a bell to a chime makes possible a great increase in the number of variations which can be performed. Thus, each new factor evolved increases the complexity of manifestation, and when the utmost diversity of which that factor renders the universe capable has been reached, that phase of evolution has reached its maximum development and there is a pause in the process while the Logoidal consciousness perceives what has taken place and 'sees that it is good', and by absorbing it into Its consciousness effects a new reaction, which reaction is, in its turn, projected into the manifested universe. So that evolution resembles a series of duplicating mirrors wherein the consciousness of the Logos projects its own image, becomes aware of and reacts to the image thus projected, and the reaction affects the projection, and so the cycle is everlastingly revolving.

You will perceive that the Logos, or subject, has become aware of an object—that object being a reflected projection, or replica, of the subject. Awareness of an external object on the part of the subject must be reproduced as a corresponding reflection of consciousness in the object; so that the object is equally capable of awareness of an external object. But the object, being of a different order of manifestation from the subject, cannot be aware of the subject but can be aware only of itself, and of the influences which proceed to it from the subject. Hence the saying, 'No man hath at any time seen God'. God cannot be seen by any unit of the manifested universe during a manifestation. He can only be deduced.

The objective awareness is not confined to any one point of the manifested universe, but is a diffused awareness around what may be conceived of as the Central Ring, metaphorically speaking; or, to use more precise but more abstract terms, those types of atoms that most nearly resemble the atoms of the Cosmic Centre, that are of the simplest type and therefore least bound by complexities, form the basis of this awareness. But let it be clearly understood that the awareness is not an atomic reaction, but is entirely of the 'force' or 'life' side of things. It is a modification of the Logoidal consciousness, not of the projected atomic consciousness. It is the first reaction in a universe which is related to that universe alone, and does not originate in, and return to, the Logos. A subject has appeared in the object.

Consciousness may be defined as reaction plus memory. That is to say, a reaction takes place in a particular type of substance, and that reaction produces a secondary reaction in another type of existence which is related to the first in the same way as the atoms of universes are related to the atoms of a Cosmos, or the 'form' of a universe is related to the consciousness of the Logos.

That is to say, the subject conceives ideas concerning itself, and these react among themselves, and the reaction, to use a metaphor, leaves a 'track in space' round which the movement of its reaction continues to flow as pure movement apart from any actual transition in space of the objects which perform the movement. That flowing of pure movement is Memory—the reproduction of an image of an action in another phase of manifestation; and consciousness is built out of memory, as distinguished from awareness which is a form of reaction between two planes.

It will thus be seen that the form or framework upon which the universe is built has been made the basis of a third type of manifestation—the manifestation of auto-reactions.

# 11.
# The Evolution of Consciousness

It is very necessary that a clear concept should be formed of the meaning of 'consciousness'; this point will therefore be elaborated.

You will recall that in teaching concerning the nature of a Great Entity it was explained that consciousness was due to the complete reciprocal reactions of all aspects of the factors and capacities for reaction that had been developed in the course of a Cosmic evolution. Consciousness is an integration of reactions, so that any change in any part is responded to by the corresponding adjustments of the whole. It is a principle of compensation that is involved, and this all-inclusive compensatory adjustment may be termed the basis of Cosmic Personality.

In its earliest phases it constitutes the synthesis of the latent reaction-capacity of an Entity. It is essentially a set of relationships, not mechanics, and is therefore abstract; but with the development of external objects that affect the Entity, new influences are brought to bear upon the compensatory adjustments, and new compensatory reactions are thus called into play.

We, then, distinguish two levels of consciousness:

(a) The basic consciousness of the inherent constitution.

(b) The compensations evoked by environmental influences.

A Great Entity, then, starts by evolving a basic nature, projects Its own image and becomes aware of that image; and Its awareness of that image in its multifarious aspects builds up the second aspect of Its consciousness. These two phases correspond to those aspects of a human being known as the Individuality and the Personality.*

* These terms are used as equivalent to 'Higher Self' and 'Lower Self' in esoteric literature.

An Individuality, whether of a Great Entity or of the microcosm which is man, is that series of organized reactions which reached an equilibrium in the preceding phases of evolution. These phases have passed away, nothing of them remains but the capacities for reaction that have been acquired by that Entity.

An Individuality, then, is a set of stereotyped reaction-capacities.

A Personality is that set of reaction-capacities which the addition of a new factor in evolution has made possible.

'Individuality' and 'Personality', then, refer to stages of development, and have a historical significance. They refer to 'time' not to 'form'. That which is the Personality today will be part of the Individuality tomorrow.

A Great Entity, then, builds up Its first Personality out of Its reaction to the Cosmic phases. It becomes conscious of the 'self' thus developed when reciprocal action of all its aspects is established. That consciousness which It thus develops is itself an existence, objective to the mind conceiving it. As soon as consciousness has focussed it as a thought-form, it is created and exists on its own account, and has become an object of consciousness; and in this thought-form, thus created, the same interplay of forces is set up which in the Cosmos gave rise to the Great Entities, and the process continues.

As the Cosmos is reproduced in miniature in the great company of Entities, by means of which its evolution is now proceeding, so the thought-form projected by a Great Entity in its turn gave rise to entities. But these entities begin their evolution at the point that the Great Entity which projects them has reached at the time of their projection. For, just as the Great Entity has latent in Itself all the phases of the Cosmos, so have they latent in themselves all the capacities of the Great Entity.

We see then in this projected thought-form of a Great Entity which we call a universe:

1. The atoms, projected by the Cosmic atoms, drawn into the orbit of that travelling atom which becomes a Great Entity.

2. The lines of force and flowing currents which are the projected consciousness of that Great Entity.

3. Out of the co-ordination established by these second-type forces among the first-type forces of the atoms, we get the setting up of currents of pure movement in space, which are the analogues of the first movement in space which gave rise to the Ring-Cosmos. Thus, evolution runs its cycle and returns upon a higher arc to the door by which it issued forth.

It is these currents of pure movement, to be clearly distinguished from the transition in space of any object, which form the basis of consciousness in the projected universe.

As before stated, action and reaction do not constitute consciousness. It is reaction plus memory which is the basis of consciousness; and the currents in space of pure movement are the basis of memory because, being frictionless because substanceless, they persist.

We have then action and reaction of manifest actions; and the persistence of the reflection of that reaction in a state which, relative to the plane upon which the reaction took place, is unmanifest. Hence the saying 'out of Chaos issues Creation.' The Unmanifest has been organized. Something exists which did not exist before. Creation has taken place. These reactions speedily affect each other and so become organized among themselves, and this reciprocal reaction is the basis of Personality. Thus, the first development of consciousness in a universe is one great and comprehensive Oversoul.

The tracks of reaction which were developed in this Oversoul by action on the planes of the atoms form invisible 'ruts' which, when any atom crosses their track, cause it to follow that course until such time as the attraction or pressure of other influences overcomes that influence.

Try and conceive of the first movement of an atom scoring a rut in 'force,' other atoms getting caught in this rut and following its curve for a time, then breaking away to follow the impulses of their own nature, and other atoms taking their place. And again, conceive the process as viewed from the plane of the atoms; you would perceive the myriad of atoms engaged in their tangential dance and from time to time you would perceive an atom suddenly change the mode of its motion, pursue the new mode for a time as if a captive under the influence of some invisible compulsion, and then break away and return to its original mode of motion. If then you examined the rut again you would find it had been worn deeper, and the next atom would be held longer before it broke away, and, as in addition to the path determined by the rut each atom dances with a movement of its own, the movement of the atom would produce modifications in the rut, and with each atom that it caught and forced to follow its path for a time, the rut would be modified. This is the first and simplest phase of the soul and the body. The tracks formed in space by gyrating atoms catch other atoms and produce secondary movements, and the track grows in consequence. The atoms which form these tracks are analogous to the travelling atoms of the Cosmos.

# 12.
# The Beginnings of Mind

We are now dealing with the beginnings of Mind, and it is necessary that these fundamentals be clearly grasped.

You have already been told that movement of any object leaves a track in space. The object comes to rest, but the movement, as apart from the object, continues as pure movement.

It is pure movement—movement in the abstract—which gave rise to the Cosmos. This movement gave rise eventually to the locked-up nodes of opposing forces which are the prime atoms. It is movement of these atoms which forms the basis of manifestation.

Manifestation, as you know it, is associated with the movement of objects, but 'Life', 'Mind', 'God', are abstract, and they are based upon pure movement unconnected with any object.

In our studies we have reached the point where the reflections of the Cosmic atoms, gathered about a Great Entity, have made the prime matter of a universe, and this prime matter has been ordered and organized into a miniature Cosmos by the reflection of the microcosmic reproduction of the Cosmic macrocosm in a Great Entity.

You will recall that in the evolution of the Cosmos the simpler types of atoms settled down upon their planes, but the more complex types of atoms could not settle down because their greater bulk caused them to react with a corresponding force to the centrifugal forces of the Cosmos, and instead of being held upon the seventh plane by the synthesis of forces, continued their outward path till they struck against the Ring-Pass-Not and were sent back to the Central Stillness.

Likewise in a universe the atoms appropriate to each plane draw their tracks in space, but because there is no persistence of action, they are mutually cancelling. These tracks form the elemental essence of each plane. But those atoms which are too complex in structure to settle down upon a plane, having gone out to the outermost plane, return thence, not to a Central Stillness but to a central point where the Unmanifest 'wells up' and becomes manifest. That is to say, it is with that phase of developing manifestation, wherein new aspects of the Logoidal consciousness are being realized, that these travelling atoms find their nearest affinity.

You will recall that it was previously said that the movement of an object leaves a track of pure movement in the Unmanifest (and remember that the Cosmic state is unmanifest when viewed from the standpoint of a universe); the Logoidal images therefore have to pass from a Cosmic to a manifest condition, and in that transition they pass through a phase which is identical with that state of existence of the tracks in space drawn by the movement of an object. Therefore, being of the same nature, they can influence the tracks in space thus drawn.

These tracks in space are always of the nature of a closed figure—like the tangential atom tracks—and as the different Logoidal concepts are externalized, these atom-tracks are influenced by them, and so reproduce in miniature the Logoidal phases. So that you can conceive great numbers of travelling atoms returning to the creative centre and being, as it were, bathed in the influences of the Logoidal ideas.

These Logoidal ideas, of course, are building the framework of the universe, and so creating a huge replica of the Great Entity, which is itself a replica of the Cosmos; but within that universe, the tracks in space of the travelling atoms, *not the atoms themselves*, are also replicas of the Logos, for the reasons given.

So that you have upon the seventh plane of a universe, gathered about the creative centre, great numbers of two-natured entities:

(a) A travelling atom which, because it has passed out through all the planes, has experienced the reactions of all the planes and therefore can react in each of these respective ways when subjected to the stimuli which produce that reaction.

(b) You also have, in addition to this atomic body, the track in space it described in its atomic dance. This track it has in common with all other atoms, but, in the case of a travelling atom which has returned to the original creative point, this track in space is impressed with the Logoidal image, and this distinguishes it from what may now be called the 'inanimate' atoms.

These atoms have come under the influence of the Logoidal self-consciousness and their tracks in space have been caused to react to that influence by the sympathetic induction of vibration, so that they have become miniature reflections of the Logos, and whereas they themselves had merely generated a tangential track of movement which had a simple rhythm of the repetition of that circular movement, they now have imparted to them by the Logoidal vibrations the same rhythm as that to which the Logos is vibrating.

Now remember that a repetition of circular movements gives rise to a rhythm and that a vibration is simply the impacting of a rhythm of one plane upon the substance of another. The Logoidal rhythms, therefore, set the travelling atoms of the universe that experience their influence vibrating to the same rhythm.

Thus it is that the travelling atoms of a universe contain the potentialities of reaction of which the nature of the Logos is capable. That is to say that the Logos—or Great Entity—in the course of Its Cosmic evolution has acquired certain types of reaction which are built into composite rhythms, and these composite rhythms are built into great chords. These chords are a series of rhythms within rhythms—loops upon loops, to use another metaphor. It is these composite rhythms that are impressed upon the travelling atoms of the universe when they approach that phase of existence where the Unmanifest is coming into manifestation, and, by the development of their own nature, they are able to contact that which is relatively unmanifest to their phase of existence.

To recapitulate, the concrete movement of an atom sets up an abstract movement of pure motion. Pure motion is the characteristic of the Cosmos and therefore is of the same type of existence as a Great Entity or Logos. So that each moving atom in the universe, by its movement, creates a counterpart of itself, of the same type of existence as that which forms the Cosmos, therefore of the same nature as the Logos of its universe, and therefore capable of reciprocal reaction with that Logos. The atoms of the planes, having settled down upon their planes, do not come into direct contact with the Logoidal mind in its realizations of concepts; the travelling atoms, however, because they have not settled down upon a plane, have not become bound to their forms—are not stabilized—and therefore return to a primitive condition after they have reached a highly evolved state, and the forces of that primitive condition cannot influence them as they can the atoms of their own plane.

These travelling atoms, then, have escaped from the laws of the manifested universe which bind into forms (for the universe itself is a thought-form) and are therefore exposed to the same laws which condition the Logoidal nature, and therefore receive an impress identical with that which the Cosmos has imprinted on the Logos—

'God made man in His image and likeness'.

Having received this imprint, these atoms proceed to gather about themselves other atoms, because the track in space, having had a definite rhythmical circular motion impressed upon it and no longer performing a cannoning tangential Brownian movement, sets up a vortex, and the vortex draws other atoms into the sphere of its movements and holds them gyrating about it.

Then you have this condition: an atom, the reflection of a Cosmic atom, which is too complex to settle down upon a plane of manifestation, returns to the Centre, having developed by its movement a circuit of pure motion which is of a Cosmic type of manifestation. Its Cosmic aspect is stamped with the Logoidal image, tuned to the Logoidal rhythm by the process described, and this abstract aspect of the atom, being thus conditioned with qualities, causes its concrete aspect to move with a circular rhythm of a corresponding type, and this circular rhythm, being thus held constant, as distinguished from the tangential movements of the atoms of the planes, sets up a vortex, and the atoms about it are drawn into that vortex.

Thus we have a Cosmic vibration of pure motion holding a travelling atom to a particular type of movement and the travelling atom, by its movement, drawing other atoms of the plane upon which this occurs into its orbit, and holding them there.

These three aspects are:

(a) The Spark of Cosmic or Divine ensouling Spirit which was first described as a track in space made by the atom.

(b) The atom, which is the beginnings of a vehicle and is known to you as the seed atom.

(c) The atoms of the seventh plane drawn into the orbit of the seed atom and constituting its seventh plane body.

# 13.

# The Evolution of the Divine Sparks

We have traced the development of a three-part unit of evolution, and you will see that three is again the number of manifestation—three Rings to the Cosmos; three aspects of a universe; and also three factors to a unit of consciousness.

These units of consciousness are each separate, in so far as the seed-atoms and those atoms of the seventh plane matter which surround them are concerned.

The seed-atom and its surrounding envelope form a definite system of stresses and reactions which are intercompensating. In their reactions to each other's stresses they have achieved an equilibrium, and have therefore become a unit.

A unit is a set of interacting forces which have achieved an equilibrium and thus become stabilized.

Such a stabilized set of interacting forces which have achieved a definite rhythm of compensation will react in unison to any outside influence, and, as no part of such a compensating system can be affected without affecting all the rest and causing them to react, it will be seen that such an association functions as a unit.

With regard to the tracks in space, however, which have received the Logoidal impress and may now be referred to as Divine Images—Reflections—Sparks from the Cosmic Fire, and which will be referred to as 'Divine Sparks', the case is different.

Let us take a single Divine Spark and study its nature.

It is exposed to three sets of influences:

1. The experiences transmitted to it by its seed-atom.

2. The influence of its fellow Divine Sparks.

3. It is *en rapport* with the Logos. It is aware of the Logos, and the Logos is aware of it.

These influences are constantly changing in rhythms of different wavelengths, and the Divine Spark endeavours by means of compensatory stresses to blend all these into a regular tune. The Logoidal influences change with the Cosmic tides which are very vast; but the influences of the seed-atom are incomparably speedier, and the Divine Spark and its fellows are all reacting without correlation to one another.

The Cosmic phases reflected by the Logoidal Mind form the first great stabilizing influences, and the warring Sparks settle down to the tides of the positive and negative phases, and gradually relationships are established, stresses are adjusted and compensated and all the Divine Sparks become correlated among themselves in a 'give and take' of reactions. When this takes place, evolution has reached its zenith.

Upon the abstract aspect they present a perfect replica of the Logos at that stage of Its evolution; and upon the 'form' side of things a geometric form is presented, built out of the atoms grouped about the nuclear seed-atoms, and this form is that to which the lines of force give rise, just as the crystal is a geometric form constructed by particles of matter arranged about lines of force. And, as the Cosmos was built up out of three inter-revolving Rings, so the Logoidal symbol is spherical; and as the number of prime manifestation is three, the symbol of the first globe is a three-sided figure—a three-sided pyramid within a sphere. You will thus perceive that the first planetary form has been evolved. Upon the Cosmic aspect of things the position has been arrived at in which a Great Entity has developed a satellite.

The Great Entity is aware of Its satellite. Its consciousness conditions Its satellite, and the satellite is aware of the Great Entity; but though the *collective* consciousness of the satellite is influenced by the Great Entity, and therefore there is reaction between Entity and satellite, it is not conscious of the Great Entity with its collective consciousness but with innumerable individualized consciousnesses whose collective consciousness is merely aware that they are aware, which is quite a different matter.

There exists, then, in the satellite, a collective consciousness which is self-conscious, aware of the conditions of its own existence as a satellite; and innumerable individual consciousnesses, which are aware of the conditions in the groups of atoms gathered around the seed-atoms with which they are associated but which are unaware of the conditions of groups of atoms gathered around other seed-atoms, and which are also each and separately aware of the Great Entity.

The consciousness of the Great Entity towards Its satellite resembles the sight of the human eye, but the consciousness of the satellite towards the Great Entity resembles the sight of a spider's eye—innumerable facets reflecting innumerable images which have to be focussed within the brain—the brain correlating with 'group-consciousness'.

When all the Divine Sparks are perfectly adjusted to each other so that there is perfect reciprocity of reaction throughout their mass, then there is a collective consciousness which focusses the images of the facets. When this is achieved there is reciprocal consciousness between the satellite and the Great Entity, because they meet on equal terms.

The form of the satellite has been determined by the Great Entity's concept of Itself, apart from the constructive consciousness of the units composing it; and now the Divine Sparks, having attained reciprocal reaction, have achieved a collective focussed consciousness, and this consciousness functions as a unit and is therefore capable of objective consciousness, and the only object of its own plane within its sphere is the Great Entity.

Now the Great Entity, being aware of the consciousness of Its satellite, is aware of that content of consciousness which is the sum total of the satellite's experiences in developing, which have already been recounted.

The Great Entity, then, has become aware of the evolution of a satellite, and this introduces a new factor into the consciousness of the Logoidal Mind, and this factor has to be assimilated to the rest of the content of consciousness; and as stability has been reached by the satellite and it has attained to a regular rhythm, the monotony of the stimulus causes the attention of the Great Entity to be withdrawn from it, and consequently freed to attend exclusively to the assimilation of the new factor which it has received into its consciousness; and the satellite, being thus without external stimulus, sinks into subconsciousness and thereby stereotypes its reactions.

The Great Entity, then, has sunk into subjective consciousness and is actively engaged in assimilating the new factor, and again achieving a synthesis of consciousness. During this process all Its forces are indrawn. It radiates nothing. It no longer holds Its Universe in consciousness. Therefore, the universe is held together only by the self-consciousness which that universe itself has achieved during the inturning of the attention of the Great Entity in the process of assimilating the new idea presented to It by Its universe.

The universe is left to its own devices and therefore does not progress or change, but constantly repeats the rhythm at which it has arrived, and thereby stereotypes it, so that the equilibrium of forces at which it has arrived at the time of the indrawing of the Great Entity's attention becomes set into a form.

The Great Entity, having thoroughly grasped and assimilated the new idea thus presented (in this case, the idea of a three-fold unit—of a travelling atom with a consciousness upon one side, and an enveloping body upon the other) rouses Itself from Its introspection to the contemplation of a universe fashioned upon this model.

The units of consciousness developed in the satellite are at once aware of the new stimulus. They are aware of the idea of action and reaction between a directing mind and an attached body, and upon this archetypal concept they proceed to evolve.

Thus, a new set of stresses is set up which oversets the equilibrium established in the group mind of that satellite, and therefore, all the units composing that satellite are dispersed, and set out to follow the path again of the wandering atoms, but plus a Divine Spark of consciousness and a seventh plane body.

The form of the archetypal satellite, however, which became stereotyped during the inturning of the Logos, remains as an archetypal form. This you may conceive as circling about the Logos upon the seventh plane.

The Divine Sparks, having progressed outwards as far as the sixth plane, by their rotary movements gather around themselves new bodies of sixth plane matter, and the process is repeated precisely as before:

(a) The re-synthesis of the Sparks.

(b) The establishment of the compensating reactions which constitutes group consciousness.

(c) The reciprocal reactions of the group consciousness and the Logoidal consciousness.

(d) The inturning of the Logos to assimilate the new idea.

(e) The stereotyping of the reactions of the satellite by repetition.

But there is this difference in the present case. During the time that the evolution of the first satellite was proceeding, there was nothing in existence in the universe save the Logos and the satellite and the planes of atoms; but during the evolution of the second satellite, the first was undergoing a new phase of development. The Logos, having realized the possibility of the endowment of atoms with the Logoidal likeness, thinks of the atoms in this way, and the atoms become thus endowed.

Now the atoms of the seventh plane, as of all other planes, are continually undergoing a backwards and forwards tide-like movement as the positive Logoidal phases draw them towards the centre, and the negative Logoidal phases thrust them outwards, and as the attention of the dim consciousness of the atoms is raised towards the Logos in Its positive phase (for, remember, that *place* in a projected thought-form universe really means *state*), the atoms receive the imprint of the Logos' concept of them, and they are thus caused to vibrate in the same rhythmical tunes as the first evolving atoms had at the time when the Logos became aware of their content of consciousness—that is to say, at the conclusion of their evolution.

The new evolving atoms thus start where the old ended. By the archetypal forces of the first satellite they are speedily sorted into the same formation as their predecessors, rapidly recapitulating their development. They have then but to arrive at a synthesis of reaction, which is collective consciousness, to become conscious of the Logos, and the same process is repeated as in the previous case.

The first swarm of atoms, having completed their evolution in the second satellite as already described, issue forth and undergo a third evolution upon the fifth plane.

The second swarm, in the first satellite, proceed likewise by the same path to the sixth plane and are there caught up and organized by the already existing set of archetypal forces left behind by the first swarm; meanwhile, as a third swarm of atoms has been sent by the Logos to people the first satellite, the Logos now thinks of atoms as having two enveloping shells, and so the new atoms are endowed with a capacity to gather about themselves matter of two planes.

Thus the process goes on until the first swarm of travelling atoms, each surrounded by an envelope of the matter of each plane upon which it has evolved, has built up a satellite upon the first plane, and each preceding satellite is peopled by hosts of Divine Sparks, each of which has built itself an envelope or series of envelopes according to the state of evolution at which it has arrived.

But as the first swarm of Divine Sparks, by the inherent forces of their natures, have devised themselves forms, the Logos has become aware of the fact and has sent out each succeeding swarm with the achievements of the first swarm implanted as archetypal *ideas* in their consciousness. That is to say whatever rhythms have been achieved are impacted as vibrations in each successive swarm.

This is what is meant by *In*volution. *E*volution is the expression of these in the matter of whatever plane it is upon which evolution is proceeding.

It will thus be seen from the foregoing that in time all the sixth plane atoms will undergo this process.

You will note that, just as the symbol of the satellite upon the seventh plane was a sphere with a three-sided solid figure—a pyramid with triangular sides, the sixth plane is a four-sided figure, a cube, and so on down the planes.

The fifth plane has a five-faceted figure. The fourth plane a six-faceted figure. The third plane a seven-faceted figure. The second plane an eight-faceted figure. The first plane a nine-faceted figure.

You will see that the numbers add up to ten, and that nine is the Number of the sides of the facets forming the figure which symbolizes the forces of the first plane. Three multiplied by three is the perfect number in the first plane.

Ten is the Number of forces in manifestation for our universe, but nine is the Number of the Cosmic force which called that universe into being when that force is manifested on the first plane.

# 14.

# The Evolution of a Planetary Being*

In the previous lecture the evolution of the Divine Sparks was traced from the time wherein all those of the same type gathered themselves together and formed a group consciousness. We then traced the phases of the development of these groups from one plane to another upon each planet, adding a shell of the atoms of that plane to the concentric layers of atoms revolving about the nucleus of the original travelling atom, until finally upon the first plane we find seven shells about the central nucleus of the Divine Sparks.

The relationship of the seed-atom, the travelling atom and the seven shells is complex, and must receive further elucidation before we proceed.

The travelling atom is a projection, not of the Logos, but of the Cosmos. It is thus at the same time more primitive and more closely related to the ultimate source of existence than a projection of the Logos could be.

The Logos projects the general framework of forces and phases which condition the universe as a whole.

The Cosmic atoms, which have come under the influence of the Logos, project the innumerable units which the Logoidal concept binds into an aggregate. The Cosmic atoms are really younger brethren of the Logos—Cosmic units themselves that have not reached the development which the Logos has reached but are of the same type. Therefore, each atom of a Logoidal universe is, for this reason, a potential Divinity.

Remember now that movement is the basis of all things. Abstract movements which are opposed lock up force and render it static, fixed. It is these locked-up forces which become 'form'. A form is simply force which is not free to move.

* In the original privately printed edition the Planetary Being was called the Planetary Spirit: the change here made gives a more accurate name.

Any series of changes which are completely compensatory settle down into a cycle of action and reaction.

As soon as such a cycle is established it cannot change its mode of motion, and therefore a force is locked up, not in a motionless point, but in a spinning ring. The points are units. The rings are organisms.

Either a unit or a ring, when once established, can move as a whole, and when this movement of an object takes place there are two factors present—the object which moves, and the movement it makes.

The movement, apart from the object, is of the same nature as the movement which gave rise to the object.

When you get an unco-ordinated movement, such as the tangential movement of the atoms before they are co-ordinated, there is no permanency of rhythm, and therefore no form is created. But as soon as compensatory co-ordination is established, forms of abstract movement are built.

This principle applies to many considerations, and is therefore elaborated here in order that it may be available for future reference, and that when the abstract archetypes of anything are referred to, you will know that it is this replica of a rhythm impacted on another plane as a vibration which is referred to. This is the key to the nature of memory.

Before proceeding further with the study of the evolution of the Divine Sparks, we will refer to the evolution of the archetypes of the globes or satellites whose origin has been described.

The unifying of the Divine Sparks into a group consciousness gave rise, as aforesaid, to the organization of their attendant atoms into the corresponding geometrical form. After the dispersal of the atoms, the archetypal *form* remains, according to the law above described.

This form is a miniature replica of the Logos under that aspect in which It is presented to Its universe, that is to say, as a system of stresses.

This system of stresses organizes the atoms of the planes on which it is into its framework, and thus equips itself with a definite form. There will then exist, in addition to the evolutionary swarm of Divine Sparks, a Planetary Being with a spherical body, built up on a framework of stresses, and this Planetary Being will be profoundly imbued with the type of activity and organization that was the characteristic of the swarm of the Divine Sparks during that phase of their evolution when they occupied its sphere.

When the next swarm comes to this phase they find that their evolution has to take place in relation to the Planetary Being, which is Lord of that sphere because it is the dominating influence thereon. They will find, therefore, ready-made the conditions which their predecessors had to evolve, and they will start therefrom upon their own evolution.

Each one, being equipped with a shell of the matter of that plane, will, from this basis, proceed to gather about it a shell of the matter of the next plane. For remember, that although in the Cosmos the planes are extended in space—being based upon movement—in a universe the atoms of the planes are not extended in space, being the products of an image held in consciousness, but are differentiated in type.

It will thus be seen that the Divine Sparks do not have to change their place in space in order to gather atoms of another type about them (because atoms of all types are everywhere) but they merely have to change their mode of motion in order to produce a type of movement in which the atoms of another plane can take part. Whenever the co-ordination of movements takes place which changes a static unit into a spinning ring of cyclic rhythm, such a change takes place, and a cyclic rhythm always gathers about it atoms of the plane below its own, because its movement approximates to theirs.

For instance, as soon as a prime atom moves along a tangential path it becomes a tangential atom. But supposing an organization of prime atoms moved along a tangential path, they would form a tangential molecule, and, being larger than tangential atoms would form a centre of attraction for these atoms, and would collect a shell of attracted atoms about them. That is how all shells are built.

To return, however, to the evolution of a Planetary Being: it will possess, to begin with, merely an organized system of the atoms of the plane on which it originated, and when the new evolutionary swarm of Divine Sparks reaches it, they would find themselves with seventh plane bodies on the seventh plane planet. But in the course of their evolution in that planet they will build themselves sixth plane shells, and they will co-ordinate their consciousness of these shells into a group consciousness, and when they depart on their evolutionary journey they will leave this group consciousness as an archetypal form in the consciousness of the Planetary Being, and this archetypal form will gather sixth plane atoms along its lines of stress, forming a second body for the Planetary Being.

This process is repeated with each fresh phase of evolution, until each Planetary Being has achieved its full complement of bodies, and is therefore able to take a swarm through the full circuit of evolution. But as each Planetary Being is profoundly imbued with the type of activity which the swarm was engaged upon when its form was a-building, each Planetary Being represents a different phase in evolution. They are therefore all different in character, and the evolutions conducted exclusively upon them have each a corresponding dominant note.

For instance, on a seventh plane planet the characteristics of the seventh plane will dominate all forms developed thereon. The prime rhythm of that plane will be the keynote, and all subsequent rhythms will be multiples of it.

In a planet upon the first plane the prime rhythm will be, likewise, the rhythm of that plane, but that rhythm, being a maximum rhythm, all subsequent variations will be fractions of it, and on the intervening planes the prime rhythms will be as decimals.

You will note that a swarm in evolution on a planet starts with the same number of bodies as that planet has, and builds an additional one in the course of its evolution, thereby endowing that planet with another body, until the maximum of seven is reached, and then devolution sets in, wherein planets and Sparks divest themselves of bodies. That subject will be dealt with later.

You will also perceive that the order of evolution in a universe is the opposite of the order of evolution in the Cosmos, because a universe is reflected from the mirror consciousness of a Great Entity. Abstract movement gives rise to forms in the Cosmos. Forms gives rise to abstract movement in a universe, and thereby link themselves on to the Cosmos, of which more later.

It is, therefore, essential in a universe to have a form in order to evolve to Cosmic level. The aim of a universe is to raise every atom to Cosmic level, thereby enabling them to link themselves on to the Cosmic atoms that gave rise to them, thereby making these Cosmic atoms into Great Entities. Thus do the atomic planes of the Cosmos evolve.

This is the secret of the divinity of man. He is related primarily not to the God of his universe Which is his Conditioner, but to his creator which is a corresponding atom in the Cosmos, which creates but has no power to condition, because it is itself conditioned by the Great Entity of which it forms a part. But when the reflected atom of a universe develops a corresponding aspect to the nature of its creator and can thereby unite with it, that Cosmic atom receives into itself all the conditions of the universe which was projected by the Great Entity of Whose body it forms a part. And, as that universe is conditioned by the Great Entity, the Cosmic atom thus becomes a replica of the Great Entity; and being thus completely conditioned by It, is no longer *being* conditioned but *has been* conditioned and therefore its conditioning is of the past, and therefore in the present it is unconditioned by the Great

Entity, because it has achieved a state in which it conditions itself, and so is independent. It is made free of the Cosmic planes, it is no longer held in bondage to the service of a Great Entity, but by means of this attachment of an evolved atom of a projected universe it is raised above the status of the atoms of its plane and becomes, in its turn, a travelling atom, and together with its attached Divine Spark of the reflected universe, it makes the round of the Rays of the Cosmos and thus, in its turn, becomes a Great Entity and develops a universe.

This is the goal of the evolution of every reflected atom in a universe—to develop a Divine Spark—to complete the evolution from the human to the Divine in a reflected universe, and to unite with its Cosmic creator, thus enabling the Cosmic atom to evolve through the phase of a travelling atom into a Great Entity.

It is this scheme of evolution we are now considering. These last details have never been revealed before. Human thought has never before passed beyond the Conditioning Logos, but it is now revealed that, though the Logos is the Creator of a universe, each atom in that universe is separately created by a separate Cosmic atom, which aspires, by means of that reflected life, to achieve a state whereby it can continue its own evolution.

Therefore, it can be said of men that, by eating of the Tree of Knowledge, they should be as Gods.

This knowledge has been withheld on the outgoing path of evolution lest souls should be tempted to turn back and forestall their goal, but to those who have passed the nadir it can now be revealed.

# 15.

# Evolution of the Lords of Flame, Form and Mind

We are now in a position to reconsider in greater detail the evolution of a Divine Spark.

Let it be noted, to begin with, that the first swarm of Divine Sparks differs from its successors in many respects.

To begin with, the first swarm is composed of the travelling atoms of the universe.

Secondly, these Divine Sparks are subjected to no other influences than those of the Logos Itself because, satellites not having been developed, they are not exposed to the influences of the Planetary Beings. Therefore, the Sparks of the first swarm have the Divine Image impressed on them in all its purity, unblurred by other influences.

There is an absence of cross-currents in the influences which play upon the first swarm which causes them to attain to the Divine Ideal with much less stress and effort than their successors. In their composition the influences of the Cosmos predominate. Each subsequent swarm, however, performs its evolution in a more highly evolved universe, and therefore the influences of the Cosmos find a potent rival in the influences of the universe.

Another point in which the evolution of the first swarm differs from the evolution of any subsequent swarm is this—the first swarm gathers the material out of which their bodies are made from the undifferentiated atoms of the plane on which they evolve; they thus carry on these atoms with them to the next globe of their evolution, and so throughout the planes. So that upon each globe upon which they evolve the potentialities of reaction corresponding to all the planes above it in the universe are established by the methods previously explained.

These Divine Sparks thus passing down the planes, leave behind them a series of archetypes, and when they pass back up the planes, by a method to be described hereafter, they become the Powers and Potencies who conduct the evolution of their successors. These are the 'Lords', the 'Principalities', the 'Regents' of whom you have heard.

The method of evolution of the subsequent swarm differs from that of the archetypal Sparks. The Logos, having received from the archetypal Sparks the concept of their evolutionary achievement, impacts this on the Divine Sparks of the second swarm by the method of vibration previously described, so that they start out on their evolution with the innate capacities for reaction laboriously built up by their predecessors, and they find themselves under the influence of a sphere of forces which the activities of the atomic portion of their predecessors formed into the sphere of a satellite.

They, in their turn, collect shells of the matter of the plane about their vortices in the course of their evolution. But there is this point of difference—they have not got to build a group mind out of their consciousness. They have merely got to attune themselves to one which already exists. They have got to become at one with their sphere, which includes the influences of the previous swarm as well as of their own swarm, and not merely at one with themselves.

When this oneness is achieved and the Logos has contemplated the result and turned inwards to Its subjective meditation these Sparks do not continue in the sphere of the satellites, as did their predecessors of the first swarm, but, the Logoidal attraction being withdrawn, the mass of the globe upon the next plane attracts them, and they are disengaged from the centripetal forces of the globe on which they are, and pass onwards.

Upon the next globe they take up the next phase of their evolution in precisely the same way as their predecessors, and again recapitulate their predecessors' behaviour up to the point of departure to the fifth plane globe.

Here a change occurs. The second swarm, having arrived at the second globe of their evolution, do not pass on to the third immediately, but are now exposed (the Logos being again withdrawn into a subjective state) to two sets of planetary influences—those of the first and third globes (the first swarm always keeping a globe ahead of them). They are therefore pulled two ways, and this conflicting influence is sufficient to overcome the attraction of the individual atoms for their atomic shells. The atomic shells then fall to pieces and return to their original condition as atoms of the plane to which they belong, but, though they are freed from the influence of the Divine Sparks, they are immediately caught up by the influences of the forces of the sphere in which that evolution has taken place, and are retained therein.

Thus upon the sixth plane, a Planetary Being will have not only the sixth plane atoms held along its line of forces, but also the seventh plane atoms shed by the Divine Sparks. A Planetary Being, be it noted, is really the conditioning influence of the life that evolves in its sphere.

The Divine Sparks that are thus deprived of their atoms, are reduced to their original state of a seventh plane atom attached to a Divine Spark, and in this state consequently re-enter the sphere of the manifesting of the Unmanifest, which, in the universe, corresponds to the Central Stillness of the Cosmos, and therein they receive anew the impress of the Logoidal Image, plus the fruits of the evolutionary achievements of the archetypal Sparks—the archetypal Sparks being always a plane ahead of their evolution.

The second-swarm Sparks always start out on their new round with potentialities of reaction of an additional plane. As they pass out through the planes they therefore gather about them the matter of each plane they pass through, forming it into concentric shells, as has been previously described, until they arrive at the fifth plane. There they build up a shell of fifth plane matter with the influence of the fifth plane planet, and repeat the processes of assimilation to the group mind, the shedding of the shells, and the return to the centre.

It will now be perceived that there is a fundamental difference between each swarm. The first swarm is engaged solely with magnetic action and reaction and vibrations, and they are called in the technical terms of occultism 'The Lords of Flame.' The second swarm is concerned with the building of matter into forms of the Planetary Beings, and they are called 'The Lords of Form.'

We will now deal with the third swarm. They issue forth, as before, seventh plane atoms, stamped with the Logoidal Image, but of a more evolved type than either of their predecessors, because the Logos has evolved by means of the evolution of their predecessors. They proceed to the planetary sphere of the seventh plane, and herein the difference of their evolution from that of their predecessors becomes apparent, for they do not collect the matter of the sphere to form a body, but use only that matter which is under the influence of the Planetary Being in whose sphere they are evolving, and as this matter is accustomed to react to an ensouling Divine Spark, it is much easier to manipulate than the matter of space. Therefore this evolution is more rapid. But as these Divine Sparks cannot advance to the globe beyond that upon which they are evolving until the preceding swarm has moved on, they are compelled to remain upon the globe of their evolution after they have exhausted its possibilities of reaction; and the superabundant energies, to which the evolving channel is closed, make play among themselves. This is the first instance of 'free will' within the Cosmos, and its resultant activities, building individualized reactions into the atoms, is called 'Epigenesis'. This is the first occasion on which the atoms are differentiated one from another, and this leads to the applying to this swarm of the name 'Lords of Mind' because individualized experience is the basis of personality.

It will here be seen that a new evolving principle is introduced—that the checking of progress in one direction enables a force to elaborate upon the original type, and lifts or sublimates it to a new aspect. If, however, the checking be too long continued it would cause it to revert to a more primitive type (this, however, cannot occur at the present phase because the synthesis of forces upon these planes is perfect, but is merely referred to in order that the correspondence may be seen). The process of evolving a new aspect of a checked force is called 'sublimation'.

The process of returning to a simpler type of evolution is called 'degradation', and is always harmful because the capacities of reaction acquired at a more advanced level cannot be controlled or checked by the governing forces of a more primitive state; they would develop an extreme individualism, thus breaking up the synthesis of force on the plane on which they find themselves.

You will, of course, perceive that it is the same type of process which sets free a travelling atom for its evolution to a higher state of existence. But a travelling atom has completed the circuit before it undergoes this experience, and may be termed 'the Child of the Cosmos'—or of the 'Universe'—as the case may be—born at full term; and the regressive, or degraded atom is one born out of due time—an abortion. If it lives at all, it lives as a monster. This is the origin of certain types of devil.

Fortunately the balances at the phase of evolution we are discussing are perfectly adjusted, because the influence of the Logos is the only influence in the universe. Therefore no such retrogression can take place among the primal swarms. It is to epigenesis in a transition state that we owe the origin of evil in a universe.

Thus the swarms pass on; the Lords of Flame leaving behind them galvanic stresses of all types, the Lords of Form leaving behind them a sediment of atoms which are built into great spherical shells by the galvanic stresses. So that each plane is dominated by a set of galvanic stresses which develop into a Planetary Being and a set of the shells of the matter of other planes held into a form or body by that Planetary Being, which develops into a planet as known to astrology. But be it noted that each planet, although it ultimately possesses matter of all seven planes, has a Planetary Being formed of the stresses of the plane on which it is.

Thus, the Planetary Being of the fifth plane would be an abstract mind; and the Planetary Being of the Earth is an etheric double.

We have now traced the three primary swarms of the outgoing arc, and you will see how each carries a new factor from plane to plane.

The first swarm—the Lords of Flame—do not return to the central point of manifestation until they have completed the round, and have been down the planes and back up the planes, and have thus completed their evolution.

The second swarm—the Lords of Form—return to the central point of manifestation only after they have recapitulated their evolution and mastered an additional plane. That is to say in their first outgoing they progress through two globes and return. In their second outgoing—through three globes and return, and so on, always following in the wake of the first swarm, with whose evolution they synchronize because as soon as the first swarm has achieved a new factor the Logos assimilates it and enters a subjective phase to do so.

During that phase, as previously said, the universe is left to its own devices. The first swarm, upon its globe, settles down to stereotype its reactions, and it is the influence of that organized globe in an otherwise unorganized universe which breaks up the shells of the second swarm in the preceding globe, and so sends them back to the central point of manifestation.

Likewise the progress of the third swarm is synchronized, because they have to wait for the second swarm to withdraw from a planet before they can advance to it. The evolution of the first swarm is slowest because it is all original work for them. The second swarm occupy much time in their evolution because they are constantly recapitulating, and gathering up, and breaking in new matter of the different planes, and therefore synchronize well enough with the progress of the first swarm. But the third swarm has much of its evolutionary work already done for it, and therefore has to wait beyond the time needed for recapitulation. Hence it elaborates itself.

Elaboration means differentiation, and differentiation means personality.

# 16.

# The Influences of the Lords of Flame, Form and Mind

Having traced the evolution of the Lords of Flame as far as the seventh globe which they form upon the first plane, we will now trace the course of their return to the centre.

It will be perceived that, by their nature, they have built those systems of magnetic stresses which constitute the framework of the globes and are afterwards elaborated into Planetary Beings. On their return journey they progress back along the line of globes by which they came out. There is this difference, however: instead of building themselves a form in the matter of a plane, they find the form already built, but they also find it inhabited by the succeeding swarm of Divine Sparks who are undergoing evolution thereon.

So that, on the sixth globe, two sets of lives are being lived—the second swarm on the outward arc, and the first swarm on the arc of returning.

The first swarm, entering into the already prepared group-mind, have objective consciousness.

The second swarm, engaged in building a group-mind, have subjective consciousness only. Therefore the Sparks are not aware of their companions of the first swarm who also inhabit this globe, though they live in their influence which has the effect of imparting to the shells of the matter of that plane which have formed about the Divine Sparks the same type of vibration as that to which the seed-atoms of the first swarm are themselves vibrating. This is the familiar phenomenon of the impactation of a cyclic rhythm inducing a vibration.

When this condition has been reached, the second swarm, being able to vibrate to the same rhythm as the first, becomes aware of the members of the first—not by direct perception, but by perception of the changes of the outermost shell induced by the presence of the first. This, however, does not occur until the end of the period of evolution, whereupon both swarms quit that planet—the second to advance to the seventh globe, and the first to return to the fifth.

In addition to the influence they exert upon their fellow sojourners in a globe the first swarm have certain evolution to undergo on their own account. On their outward journey they have collected to themselves shells of each plane, which they have not shed but have carried out with them. And on the return journey each shell forms a means of reaction to the matter of each plane on which they find themselves. Being capable of both action and reaction these form vehicles of manifestation and means of perception.

Thus the indwelling Spark is able to act on, and react to, the matter of each plane on which it finds itself, and though it carries out its evolution in the sphere of attraction of the globe on that plane, it can yet extend its activities a certain way beyond the sphere of the influence of that globe. This is a point whose significance will be seen later.

Upon each globe on the return journey the Sparks of the first swarm exercise their influence upon the shells that are being gathered about the Sparks of whatever swarm they encounter there. Upon the sixth globe they meet the second swarm: when they themselves depart to the fifth globe the third swarm advances to the sixth globe, and so on. This causes the first and the third swarms just to miss each other. Therefore the third swarm is distinguished by this peculiarity—it never meets the Lords of Flame: it never encounters an evolution higher than its own, and therefore its predominating influence is that of the Logoidal Image, and of the production of its own 'epigenesis'. That is why 'Mind' has so much freedom, as compared with 'Form' or 'Force'.

It will be seen that, as each swarm except the third meets the Lords of Flame on a different planet, it is a different shell that is influenced by those Lords. This accounts for the differences in the organization of the vehicles upon the different 'Life Waves'. It is a point closely connected with practical magic, because whatever body has received the impress of the Lords of Flame, that body will be used in working upon Nature Forces.

The Lords of Form, likewise, when developing upon a globe, exert a similar influence upon their fellow-sojourners there, but being peculiarly and intimately related to the matter of that globe, their inter-reaction with the shells of the Sparks of the junior swarm is peculiarly intimate.

When, however, the Lords of Mind have passed the nadir and begin to return up the globes, conditions of evolution are much complicated, because the freedom of individual action of their Divine Sparks has been enormously developed by successive periods of 'epigenesis', and in their diversity of reactions they produce the diversity of development in the swarms they contact.

We have traced the progress of the first three Life Swarms as far as the first plane. We will now trace the mode of their return up the planes.

It will be recalled that the Lords of Flame complete the full cycle before returning to the sphere of divine influence wherefrom they issued.

The Lords of Form evolved by means of a gradually lengthening series of journeys. In the first journey they progressed as far as the sixth plane and returned again to the sphere of divine influence. In the second journey they progressed through two globes to the fifth plane, and so on down the planes until, on the sixth journey they reached the first plane. It will thus be perceived that upon the final journey of their outgoing they have already within themselves the capacities of reaction of all the planes, and have nothing further to acquire in that respect. They have, however, to learn the lessons of the return journey, which will be dealt with in their place.

The evolution of the Lords of Mind resembles that of the Lords of Flame in that it is a continuous journey, but at each pause, while they wait their turn for progress, they make original additions to the sum of factors of their reactionary complex.

It will have been noted that, from the time the first swarm sets out upon its homeward journey, two types of evolution will always be progressing in a globe at the same time, and the senior evolution profoundly influences that aspect of the junior evolution which corresponds to its own nature. This is the prototype of the process known as initiation.

These matters cannot be dealt with in detail until other aspects of the subject have been considered. They will then be reverted to.

It will be remembered that upon each plane the Divine Sparks acquired a fresh mode of reaction. They learnt of a plane, but were limited by the conditions of that plane. Upon the return arc they are not seeking to penetrate into, and master, the conditions of a fresh plane as a means of evolution but to withdraw from a plane and thus to free themselves from its limitations while at the same time retaining the capacities for reaction they learnt thereon. This freedom can be obtained only after the complete synthesis of reactions of that plane has been achieved by the group spirit of the swarm.

The synthesis is so complete that the reactions, being mutually compensating, become automatic and demand no individual compensating. Habitude renders them subconscious, and the consciousness of the Sparks being directed to the reactions of a higher plane, they function according to the type of that plane, and their reactions are such that the atoms of the lower plane can no longer accommodate themselves thereto and therefore are dispersed. In this way the Lords of Flame withdraw up the planes.

The Lords of Form progress by a different type of evolution. For each lesson they learn they teach to the Logoidal Consciousness before progressing further, and they await the impact of the Logoidal Image which is the evolutionary impulse which sends them forth on their next journey. When they have been out to the uttermost plane and returned for the sixth time, they have given their final message to the Logoidal Consciousness; and the seventh journey which, as far as they are concerned is a repetition, can add nothing new to the Logoidal Consciousness. It is their function, however, upon each globe, to make a contribution to the forces of formation in the manifested universe. Their essential type of reaction is the stereotyping of forms, and they influence profoundly the atoms that are built into the body of the Planetary Being of each globe.

The Lords of Flame influence the evolving Life-Sparks of each globe they are on. The Lords of Form leave them untouched, but influence the globe itself. Were it not so this stereotyping of form would prevent evolution in the Divine Sparks. As it is, the stereotyping of form in the vehicles of the Planetary Beings has determined in them the most primitive type of vehicle of manifestation—the sphere—an inorganic secretion of matter around a nucleus of attraction. It is the Lords of Mind who exert the predominating influence on the swarms they contact on each plane, because, owing to the fact that they have achieved individualization, they are able to act upon individual Sparks, and are not merely obliged to influence a group mind through a general atmosphere.

# 17.

# The Lords of Mind as Initiators

It is a peculiarity of all vibratory objects that they tend to tune with their own vibrations all objects of a slower rhythm than themselves, being limited in this activity only by the vibrationary capacity thus influenced. Whereas the Lords of Flame were limited in their power to raise vibrationary activities by the sum total of the group-reaction, the Lords of Mind, should individual junior Sparks show special reactionary capacities, are able to raise them individually. The Sparks thus developed exercise a profound influence on the Life Swarm of which they form a part, for they are initiates.

On the outgoing arc of evolution, initiation is performed by contact with the life of a swarm on the returning arc.

Thus, initiation on the outgoing arc enables the initiate to cut across the arc of evolution, and to obtain the reactionary capacities by sympathetic induction, instead of by the lengthy process of experience. Initiation upon the returning arc is, however, a different process which will be considered in due course.

The function of initiates on the outgoing arc is to enable their swarms to adapt themselves more speedily to the conditions of a newly-achieved plane, because they have acquired some concept of the nature of these conditions. Thus, initiation on the outgoing arc enables an initiate to immerse himself more rapidly in matter.

Let us now consider the conditions of the first swarm when it returns once more to the sphere of divine influence.

It issued forth as a cloud of Sparks. It returns as an organized set of magnetic, capillary, centrifugal, centripetal, and vorticular stresses, with a mass momentum.

The Logos is then confronted by an organization that approximates in influence to Its own. Whatever reactions the Logos might now impose upon Its universe could encounter the organized opposition of the first swarm. The Logos, however, works not in opposition to that which It has Itself created, but acts as a synthesizer between the Cosmos by which It is influenced and the organization which now forms a conditioning influence in Its universe. By Its perception of this organization a corresponding image arises in Its consciousness, and the Great Entity is thus conditioned by the conditions of Its universe, and therefore all Cosmic influences are transmuted under the influence of that conditioning before they are communicated to the universe.

The Logos has now acquired the same reactionary capacities, by contemplation of the evolved swarm, that the swarm acquired by experience of the planes. Therefore the Great Entity and Its manifestation vibrate synchronously, and are at one; and, after a period of compensating action and reaction, they evolve a rhythm. The Logoidal vibrations are extended to the Group Spirit of the swarm, and the Group Spirit of the swarm is absorbed in the consciousness of the Great Entity. The individualized Sparks, however, maintain their individuality, but their Group Spirit is no longer a separate entity, for the consciousness of the Great Entity has become at one with it, and therefore it is at one with the Logoidal consciousness, so that the Oversoul of the swarm is the Logos Itself. This is the goal of evolution of a Life Swarm—the assimilation of the Group Spirit to the Logoidal consciousness whereby the Logos receives the fruits of its evolution.

It may now be asked 'Whither go the Sparks?'

In the case of the Lords of Flame they are so completely withdrawn from the manifested universe that they cease to be upon the planes of manifestation, but remain at the central point of impactation, maintaining a balancing action and reaction between the manifest and unmanifest.

Some, however, succeed in making contact with their corresponding atoms, and these pass out of the sphere of Logoidal evolution to experience the life of a travelling atom in the Cosmos. Those that do not so proceed remain as conditioning influences in the universe, and, being at one with the Logoidal Mind, are able to execute the Logoidal Will. The forms which they built in the course of their evolution form part of the frame-work of the universe, and as such are stereotyped. But whenever the Logos desires to effect compensatory actions in response to the unco-ordinated stresses of an evolving universe, it is by means of the Lords of Flame, thus freed from the bonds of manifestation, that this is achieved. 'And He made His ministering Spirits a flame of fire', and 'Flames of fire were His ministering Spirits'. The Lords of Flame are concerned with the basic natural forces.

The Lords of Form, likewise, on completing their evolution, undergo similar adjustments, and when the Logos, having received a new concept from an evolving swarm, desires to impress an archetypal concept upon a swarm in process of evolution, it is the Lords of Form who are employed for the process. Their method we will study later.

The Lords of Mind, likewise, upon their return are assimilated to the Divine consciousness, and employed as mediators between the Logos and Its universe.

Now, be it recalled that the Lords of Mind established individualization, and they deal essentially as individuals with individuals, whereas the Lords of Form deal with Group Souls.

The Lords of Mind are the initiators of our present evolution, and as such will receive much reference in the course of these teachings. They it is who, able to react upon all planes of manifestation, range up and down the planes, performing adjustments by exercising compensatory stresses when the faculty of epigenesis has disordered an evolution.

Upon the plane where they function they are simply centres of force, therefore they are unperceived by the denizens of that plane. They can, however, by the assistance of a vehicle of that plane, detach certain elements to form nuclei for the building of vehicles in the matter of that plane; hence the concept of the 'Virgin Birth.' And therefore it is that those who are known as the 'Saviours' are always represented as born of agamogenesis. They bring their own life impulse; nothing but the accretion of matter is required for their manifestation.

In this outline we have traced the development of a manifested universe up to the point where the Divine Sparks of the prime swarms have returned to the Logos—achieved union, and function as intermediaries between the Logos and Its universe.

It will be recalled that the Logos has three prime aspects. Each of the three prime swarms was projected into manifestation under an impulse of one of the prime aspects of the Logos, and may therefore be regarded as the representative of that aspect to the universe. These three prime manifestations are of a different degree from all others.

It will thus be seen that each of the Primary Swarms after it has achieved oneness with the Logos, performs the part of 'Compensator' or 'Counterpoise' in the work of evolution, for, with the coming in of epigenesis, comes also the risk of developments out of harmony with the Logoidal nature. Likewise, these evolved swarms are employed to convey to the outgoing Sparks the fruits of evolution that have been achieved, and thus save a needless recapitulation of reactions already stereotyped in the universe.

Subsequent Life Swarms develop under the influence of the Logos plus the Regents, and as, in addition to the three prime aspects derived from the Rings of the Cosmos, the Logos also reacts to the influence of the twelve Cosmic Rays, all subsequent evolutions are characterized by the influence of the Rays which predominated at the time that they, the subsequent swarms, received the Logoidal impulse.

As these Cosmic impulses are received by the Logos by means of Zodiacal initiations, the Group Spirits of the swarms thus developed are known as the 'Ray Exemplars'.* These are closely concerned with types in the evolving Sparks.

We have now concluded a description in outline of the evolution of the Logos and Its Regents who condition all succeeding evolutions.

* Called 'Star Logoi' in the original edition; changed here as the term Exemplar is more apt.

# 18.

# Influences Acting on Human Evolution

We are now considering the influences under which human evolution takes place:

*Logoidal Influences*

(a) Cosmic influences acting on the Logos—the Rings, the Rays as exemplified by the Zodiac, and other Great Entities.

(b) Modifications of the Logoidal Consciousness produced by reactions to the evolution of the manifested universe.

*Influences of the Manifested Universe*

(a) Plane conditions.

(b) Influences of Ray Exemplars.

(c) Influences of Planetary Beings.

(d) Influences of other evolutions sharing the same planet.

*Factors of the Manifested Universe*

These factors are stereotyped types of reactions which always function on appropriate occasions. Being built up by preceding evolutions, they form the inheritance of each subsequent evolution and are innate capacities. There are very many of them. We will enumerate certain of the major ones:

1. Law of action and reaction—equal and opposite.

2. Law of the aspects of force, or polarity.

3. Law of impactation, or transmission of action from one plane to another.

4. Law of the attraction of the Centre.
5. Law of the attraction of outer space.
6. Law of limitation.
7. Law of the Seven Deaths.

Under the influence of these factors, of which the above are some of the principal, evolution proceeds, and to terms of these factors it can be reduced.

The Logoidal influence predominating at the time that a new phase is being developed determines the type of life or vehicle evolved.

**Cosmic Influences**

You are accustomed to the concepts of astrology which delineates the planetary influences affecting the Personality. The subject of our discussion is the Cosmic influences affecting the Individuality, which may be termed sidereal astrology in distinction from planetary astrology.

The universe evolves subject to the determining influence of the Logoidal consciousness, and the Logoidal consciousness experiences in its turn the influences of the Cosmic Tides. Therefore the universe is modified indirectly by the action of the Cosmic Tides.

The Cosmic Tides consist of the influences of the positive and negative phases of the Rings. These phases affect the Cosmos as a whole, so that the twelve Cosmic Rays and the seven Cosmic Planes function with their positive and negative aspects alternately predominating. This means that when the positive phase predominates, the forces of action—the apex shall we say—may be conceived of as in the centre. When the negative predominates, the apex is at the circumference.

Thus in a positive phase a circuit would consist of an inflowing and an outgoing: in a negative phase, of an outgoing and an inflowing. The action of a Ray, therefore, differs greatly according to whether it be experienced under a positive or negative phase of the Rings, so that a Great Entity may be conceived of as circling round the Cosmos in Its orbit, and receiving the influence of the Rays as It passes through their areas, but receiving it alternately under their positive and negative aspects.

The evolution proceeding in the universe will be correspondingly modified according to whether that evolution takes place when the Logos is experiencing a positive or negative Cosmic influence.

The calculating of these influences constitutes sidereal astrology. This is the astrology which relates to the lives and fates of Group Souls and

Planetary Beings. It concerns the nativities of the heavenly bodies themselves. The basis of this calculation is the precession of the equinoxes.

The equinoxes and the Cosmic Ray phases correlate and there are four phases to a Ring phase. On that basis you can calculate out the sidereal influences affecting evolution. Remember this, however, that these influences do not affect human lives directly, but affect the Planetary Beings which, in their turn, influence the mental and 'karmic' atmosphere in which a soul reacts; and the Planetary Beings themselves are modified by the tracks in space described about them by the evolution of a group soul of any life swarm that is progressing through their sphere: so that, although the Logoidal influences are immutable, modifications are introduced in the course of transmission.

Thus the astrology of the ancients, though fundamentally true, is not strictly accurate at the present day. The developments caused by evolution must be allowed for. Therefore, those aspects which in primitive times might be interpreted as war and bloodshed, at the present time might be interpreted as a conflict of ideas.

Sidereal astrology should always be calculated in relation to the race before any horoscope of an individual of that race is cast. Group minds and group souls are subject to sidereal astrology; individuals to planetary astrology plus sidereal astrology.

Work out the equinoctial positions. From that you can calculate the Ring influence. This will enable you to know whether the Heavenly House is in its positive or negative aspect, and this will tell you what aspect of the Logos is in function. Whatever aspect be thus energized will stimulate the corresponding aspects in all manifestation.

Breaking down and building up aspects depend on the Cosmic Rings, and the particular form of destruction or construction depends on the Cosmic Ray. Those prime conditions underlie all others and frequently falsify the best-made calculations.

In addition to these regular and calculable influences of the Cosmos there are the irregular influences caused by the passing of other Great Entities upon other planes of the Cosmos, as previously referred to. You will find the particulars on this subject in a previous chapter.

There is no method which you are capable of grasping whereby such influences can be reduced to a calculable system, but they correlate with the approach of comets. Some, therefore, are known to you, for some of the comets have had their orbits calculated. Some are still unknown to human thought, but give adequate notice of their approach by the disturbances induced in other heavenly bodies.

The astrology of the comets has been but little worked out and would repay attention. The best method of calculation is through the spectroscopic record of a comet. This will enable its chemical composition to be deduced, and the proportions of the elements will give the necessary clue to its nature, especially the proportion of the metals, which, being referred to their appropriate correspondences, will furnish the key to the problem of good and evil, the fruit of the Tree of Knowledge.

Thus it can be seen of which aspect the force is the support or pillar, for that which it supports will have its activity intensified, so that that which might be expected to be a negative phase may unexpectedly become positive.

The basis of calculation of sidereal astrology, then, is the equinoxes, subject to the irregular modifications of other Great Entities.

The comets it may be said, are aggregates of atoms drawn together by means of the electrical disturbance occasioned by the influence of Entities upon subtler planes. These Entities are great cosmic beings that have no matter of the seventh Cosmic plane in their composition and therefore cannot form a universe which is perceptible to the physical senses of the first plane of a Solar evolution.

The comets do not generate a group soul *which can evolve.* They are 'Sidereal Idiots.' Artificial Elementals are their souls, and they are concerned—certain of them—with Cosmic scavenging. To them are sent those rare units of an evolution which, by the persistent misuse of epigenesis, have dedicated themselves to destruction. The comet in its orbit takes such souls to the outermost bounds of the Cosmos wherein there are no influences to which they can react, and the Cosmic atom-images which go to the building of their component parts cease to be reflected.

That is the 'Unknown Death.' Such units cease to be—completely—and there is no reincarnation or fresh start. Even their karma is disintegrated and touches not the Group Spirit. It is said of such that they exchange their planet for a comet. They elect to go far and fast, but they go too far and too fast for their forces of cohesion, and the comet to which they have yoked themselves when it returns again to the sphere of our solar system is found to be without them.

Solar evolutions proceeding from the Solar Logos synchronize roughly with the Ring influences of the Cosmos. That is to say that under the positive Cosmic influences the Logos will give the stimulus which sends a new swarm upon its journey, but the length and speed of that journey synchronize thenceforth with nothing else because there are so many counteracting influences, but it will have to make its passage through the nadir at a time when the Cosmic Tides are turning. But it may have one or many Cosmic phases upon its outgoing arc. The change of a phase will always precipitate an evolutionary crisis, but when an evolution is approaching the limit of its developmental capacities it will not venture over the dead-centre until a Cosmic Tide-turn occurs, but will perform epigenesis and bide its time.

Those beings which essay the task of passing the nadir under unfavourable influences and fail to make the transition, revert along the original path when the Cosmic Tide comes later, and become demons and devils. Hence the distinction of the 'Left-hand Path'.

The Left-hand path can be gained in two ways—by deliberate crossing of the arc from right to left after the nadir has been passed, or by a retroversion before the nadir has been passed.

You will see by this that it is necessary to watch the Cosmic Tides when undertaking any regenerative work in relation to the spiritual guidance of humanity.

The great constructive period of the nineteenth century afforded a valuable starting ground for many spiritual impulses. The first quarter of the twentieth century was a phase of destruction.

# 19.
# The Logoidal Relation to the Manifested Universe

It will be realized from the study of the foregoing chapters that the Logos is related subconsciously to the Cosmos and consciously to the universe. Remembering also that the Logos is affected by the positive and negative Cosmic phases, you will perceive that under the negative influence Its consciousness will tend to subjectivity and therefore the Cosmic influences will predominate in the Logoidal consciousness. At the same time, the Logoidal influences will be withdrawn to a great extent from the manifested universe, which will be left to the control of the forces which it has itself generated in the course of its evolution.

These periods are referred to as the 'Days and Nights of God'. Be it noted, however, that there are the 'Greater' and 'Lesser' Nights and Days.

The relation of the Logos to Its universe will best be realized by remembering that a phase of evolution is to the Logos what an incarnation is to a man.

The forthsending and returning of an evolutionary life swarm conveys the same harvest of experiences to the Logoidal Consciousness as the Individuality of a man receives from the incarnation of a Personality.

The Logos Itself corresponds to the Divine Spark.

The Universe, in its Group Soul aspect, corresponds to the Individuality.

The evolutionary swarm corresponds to the Personality.

Bearing these correspondences in mind, you will be able to interpret the Logos in the light of man, and man in the light of the Logos.

The formation, development, and devolution of a universe correspond to the evolutionary cycle of the Logos, so that the Logos develops by means of a series of incarnating impulses, which are the evolutionary life-waves or swarms.

Each succeeding wave of evolution penetrates deeper into the 'form' aspect of the universe; renders it more complex in its organization; brings it a stage further in the development of that perfect balance of forces which it seeks to reach as a whole, and when the entire manifested universe reacts as a whole it is fully self-conscious. As soon as self-consciousness is established, objective consciousness becomes possible. The universe then becomes aware of the Logos, and reciprocal consciousness between Logos and universe is established.

We have then, first, the self-conscious Logos. Secondly, in order that the Logos may establish objective consciousness, the need of an object of which It can be conscious. The Logos, therefore, projects Its concept of Itself and becomes conscious of that.

The concept, in its turn, develops self-consciousness through successive phases of evolution. The Logos is aware of these changes as they take place, and is modified by the knowledge.

Finally, the universe, having attained full self-consciousness, becomes objectively conscious and is aware of the Logos. But as the Logoidal consciousness has developed, step by step with a universal consciousness, they are identical, the only distinction being that the Logos has a background of Cosmic conditions, and the universal consciousness has a background of mundane conditions.

The Logos, then, absorbs into Itself the universal consciousness, because the Cosmic forces, by their attraction, overcome the cohesion of the mundane forces.

All these systems of organized reactions, which held together the atoms of the manifested universe, are therefore withdrawn from the planes of the manifested universe into the Cosmic state of existence, and the atoms, of which the manifested universe was composed, return to their primary condition of tangential movement, unco-ordinated by any superior force. This is the Lesser Chaos, and is referred to expressively as 'Old Night' or the 'Night of the Ages'.

It will be seen, then, that the goal of evolution is the development of a consciousness which can unite with the Logoidal consciousness and pass from the phase of a reflected, or a projected existence—a phenomenal existence—to that of a real, actual or noumenal existence in the Cosmic state. This can be achieved only when the entire manifested universe is perfectly synthesized. This represents the 'Pralaya' or 'Night of God'.

A lesser 'Night', however, occurs at the completion of each phase of evolution during the time in which the Logos meditates upon the concepts presented to It as the fruits of that evolution, thereby modifying Its own consciousness. And each succeeding swarm of Divine Sparks receives the impression of the modified Logoidal consciousness, as previously explained, and therefore starts upon its evolution with an elaborate reaction-capacity already developed.

The matter of each plane, having been used to build forms of a certain type, retains the reaction-capacity of that type after the forms have been disintegrated, and therefore assembles into similar forms with a greater readiness each time it is called upon to repeat the process until finally it holds these forms of its own organized forces. Thereby subsequent life-waves are compelled to assume these forms and are conditioned thereby. This is retrogressive, because each life-wave, having performed epigenesis, is more highly elaborated than its predecessor, and therefore cannot enter the same mould without deformity.

It must, then, be realized that each unit of a life swarm has, inherent in its nature, the reaction-capacities of the Cosmos in its simplicity, and of all preceding life swarms in their complexity. Therefore, though fundamentally it has a perfect simplicity of principle, it has an infinite complexity of reaction-capacity.

The Cosmic principles are known and constant. To these each human soul is obedient as to the fundamental laws of its nature. But the reactions of epigenesis cannot be calculated in relation to individuals because of their complexity and the number of possible modifying factors. They can only be calculated in relation to evolutions because the number gives the average.

Hence it is that epigenesis introduces the element known as 'free will', and free will, in the interval between its development and its synthesis with the Logos, gives rise to the 'positive' evil of the manifested universe.

# 20.

# Influences of the Manifested Universe

The teaching of the last two lectures was devoted to a consideration of the extra-universal influences. We are now in a position to consider the intra-universal influences.

Let it be borne in mind that the extra-universal influences are of two types:

First, the Cosmic influences which act upon the Logos, and to which the Logos reacts, thus undergoing changes which are reflected upon the manifested universe as variations and phases of the Logoidal influences. The Logoidal influences are therefore not constant, though true to type. This is an important point in which esoteric theology differs from exoteric theology which conceives of God as changeless, whereas esoteric theology conceives of God as Himself evolving, and as subject to mutation according to law.

Secondly, the Logoidal influences change owing to manifestations in the Logoidal nature produced by Its reactions to the evolution of the universe. Thus we may say that the Logoidal influences playing upon the manifested universe vary in these two ways, and these have to be reckoned with in all calculations of the influences to which evolving humanity is subject, and they can be calculated:

(a) in the Cosmic type—by means of the equinoxes and the comets;

(b) in the evolutionary-reaction type—by calculating the curve and studying the phases of biological history.

We will now proceed to deal with the conditions in the manifested universe subject to which man carries on his evolution.

It will have been perceived from a study of the foregoing chapters that all action and reaction which is regular becomes cyclic, according to the law of universal curvature; and that cyclic reaction makes a 'track in space' and thus becomes stereotyped. Therefore the manifested universe is at any given time a set of molecules and atoms held together by a framework of 'tracks in space'. In other words, the organized manifestations of the 'One Existence' are simply a set of stereotyped reactions of which the 'tracks in space' form the abstract mould. (The idea of the 'abstract mould' is an important one and should be borne in mind.)

These sets of stereotyped reactions are of many different types, and they can be distinguished according to the mode of their origin. Some were left behind by the Lords of Flame in the course of their evolution; others by the Lords of Form; others by the Lords of Mind; and each of these sets of stereotyped reactions forms the Natural Law which govern the manifestations of those particular kinds of forms and activities which were built up in the course of that evolution, and these form the distinctions between one kind and another. But as each evolution makes use of the creations of its predecessor, the reaction types of that predecessor will be found inherent in the successors, though the analytical mind can dissect them not. They also, however, all exist as independent sub-strata, and it is the knowledge of the methods of manipulating these, the elemental essences of each kingdom, which is the basis of practical magic; and remember that each type of manifestation has its elemental essence.

You will recall that each phase of the manifested universe was built up in turn, and that these phases form the fields of development of subsequent life-waves. It therefore follows that each life-wave, at each phase of its evolution, will be conditioned by the conditions of the plane upon which that phase is undergone. Therefore an understanding of the planes is essential to an understanding of the problems of evolution, and of Initiation (which is simply condensed evolution).

The laws of the first or physical plane are being worked out by means of the five physical senses which relate to that plane, and are well known to you under the generic name of Natural Science, though why man should consider one of the planes of his existence 'natural' and the rest 'unnatural' is a strange fruit of epigenesis! These conditions, so far as the inanimate world is concerned, have been well and truly observed, and subject to these laws life will proceed with its evolution upon the physical plane. But scientific thought has made a mistake in believing that these laws are all there are, and this mistake has vitiated the last hundred years of science. The ancients were wiser, though not so well informed. Certain schools of religious philosophy, however, make the opposite mistake and believe that life can work out its evolution regardless of the laws of the physical plane. This is also a mistake.

The forces of a plane are supreme upon their own plane, controllers of the plane below, and, when in contact with the plane above, are in their turn controlled.

For example, the laws of logic are supreme in the realm of mind. The images of mind control the forms of the emotions, but the images of mind are themselves controlled by the spiritual forces.

Each plane is capable of independent function, or of function in circuit, but as soon as the planes are put in circuit it is necessary that the current should be completed by uniting the arc upon the seventh plane, otherwise the open arc will short-circuit to the Left-hand Path.

For example, should the trained mind learn to control the body of emotions, and the body of emotions learn to control the physical vehicle, you have an arc in function of which one half is conscious, or negative, and the other half sub-conscious, or positive, and the sub-conscious always gives the stimulus. If that arc be not completed into a circuit by junction through the Logoidal Image on the seventh plane, it will short-circuit from conscious to sub-conscious upon the fourth or fifth according to type; and the sub-conscious, being the positive or stimulator, will assume the control.

Now the sub-conscious was built up in the past. Therefore the past will assume control. That man will then return to an earlier phase of evolution, and will be actuated by its motives while retaining the faculties of a later form of evolution.

Though these motives were adequate to the control of the simple faculties of that phase, they are inadequate to the control of the complex faculties of a later phase, and that man becomes a danger to evolution by destroying the poise of the group soul of which he is a member, and as, it will be remembered, it is a function of the Entities evolved in earlier life-waves to adjust the balance of compensating forces of the universe, he will be dealt with by the Destroyers, and will be reduced to his lowest common denominator. That is to say, his later faculties will be taken from him, and he will be left only with those faculties suitable to his impulses. Certain types of mischievous malicious idiots are produced in this way.

The doctrine of the planes cannot be understood without the doctrine of the Planetary Beings.

Let it be remembered that a Planetary Being was evolved with the development of each plane, but that as the Planetary Being itself was developed at the time that the plane was being evolved, its highest self will be the subtlest aspect of the matter of that plane. Thus the subtlest aspect of the Earth is etheric. It is a plane of forms without intelligence.

Each Planetary Being then is the Archetype of the life of its plane, and is the great dominating influence of that plane. In the course of the evolutionary tides, however, matter of the planes below is gathered about that Planetary Being, thus forming shells or bodies for it; but matter of the planes above is not so accreted. For these elements in its nature it depends upon the influences from superior planes which act upon its atmosphere, and that element in its atmosphere is more directly supplied by the corresponding aspects in the lives inhabiting its sphere.

Thus the Planetary Being is as a Group Soul of that plane on which it functions, through the planes below it to the dense physical, with which it has been supplied; but the elements of the plane above it, which serve it as Individuality, are supplied by the lives evolving in its sphere, and partake of the nature of a Group Mind of the life of that planet. This is a subtle but important distinction, for it means that the Higher Self of the Planetary Being depends upon the lives dwelling on it for its development.

A Planetary Being is a vast Artificial Elemental for which humanity builds a Greater Self, and while the Planetary Being determines the conditions of all evolution and all function within its sphere, the higher aspects do not belong to it but are related to those Planetary Beings who are its seniors.

Therefore, it is that, in relation to the Earth, the man who would attain the maximum evolution within her sphere—who would achieve the supreme humanity of the animal aspect—must make himself at one with the forces of the Earth and of her subtle self—the Moon. But it is only by the influences of the higher planets that he can raise consciousness to the higher planes, and upon the tides of the planets he must make the transition.

He who takes the Earth as his planet becomes earthbound and the time is soon now, as Cosmic time is reckoned, that the present human evolution will be withdrawn from the Earth plane, and therefore the advanced souls of that evolution do not find their development in communion with the Earth Soul. It is to the children of the Elements that the Earth is an Initiator, not to the children of men. The Earth and the Moon Initiations are physical Initiations and concern the 'fall' into matter and generation.

The planets may be assigned as follows:

The Earth to the plane of the dense physical.
The Moon, her satellite, to that division of it known as the etheric.
Mars dominates the plane of the instincts and passions.
Venus is the planet of the abstract emotions.
Saturn is the planet of the concrete mind. Saturn, be it noted, is the formative influence.
Mercury is the planet of the abstract mind.
Jupiter is the planet of the concrete spiritual.
The Sun itself is the symbol of the Logos on the seventh plane.

Conceive, then, each 'planet' as the Archetype of its plane; as radiating out its influences upon that plane, and tuning that plane to its vibrations. And conceive each evolution as developing the corresponding factors within its nature when sojourning on a plane on the outgoing arc, and upon the returning arc aspiring to dominate those factors within itself and thereby to dominate the condition of the plane by means of the rapport thus developed with its ruling influence. The domination can only be completely achieved by securing the sympathetic co-operation of the Planetary Being.

Now, as has been aforesaid, the Planetary Beings are great but mindless Entities, therefore each has assigned to it a Guide; and these Guides are of the first evolution—being Lords of Flame; and they are called 'Archangels of the Spheres'. It is through them that the dominion of the planes is secured.

These Archangels of the Spheres have their own Initiates who know the 'consonants of the Names', and they are concerned with the evolution and regeneration of the planets to which they are assigned—as the Masters are concerned with the Earth plane.

The Ray Exemplars are not the Planetary Beings, but represent the Zodiacal influences of the Cosmos upon the solar system. These influences, likewise, are built up as Artificial Elementals to whom are assigned Archangelic Guides. But the Rays, being older than the Planes, are more highly evolved, and instead of being overshadowed, as are the Planetary Beings, in their case identification is complete. The Ray Exemplars are Lords of Mind.

The Elemental aspect of each Ray Exemplar is built up by the evolution which takes place under its influence, and a Ray Exemplar might be termed the Group Mind of that evolution. Each evolution builds a Ray Exempler and thereby, as it were, focuses, stereotypes and tames that particular aspect of the Cosmic influences through which it evolves.

These Ray Exemplars remain in function after the Cosmic Tide which called them into being has passed away, and thereby the Cosmic influences of that type are maintained in function in the universe which evolution is developing into the form of a miniature Cosmos.

Finally there remain to be considered the influences of other forms of life—evolutions of a later and an earlier day in process of development. In the normal way these do not influence each other at all, but, being of different states of consciousness though perchance occupying the same globe, have no point of contact; but under certain conditions contacts may be established, and these contacts are popularly known as 'psychism.'

Psychism is of two types: (a) the perception of that which is below in point of evolution; and (b) the perception of that which is above; and the Earth, being at the nadir, these two ways of seeing may be conceived of as looking back along the Left-Hand Path, or forward along the Right-Hand Path. It is permissible to look forward as far as the eye can range, because that will lead the soul forward, for where the eye looks the feet will turn.

We may never look backward up the planes; and we can only look across the planes from the involutionary to the evolutionary arc. Thus it is that those Entities which dwell upon or raise their consciousness to, shall we say, the third plane, may minister unto those in their sphere who are upon that plane on the outgoing arc, but those upon the physical plane may not look at the involutionary aspect of a subtler plane until they have mastered its evolutionary aspect.

The Initiators of the physical plane are those who have attained perfection on the seventh plane. Initiators always function across the diameter (upon a diagram you will see the significance of this) and the seventh initiates the first. Therefore, man upon Earth is bidden to worship—not the Nature Forces of the second plane, nor the Saints of the third, nor the Masters of the fourth, nor the Angels of the fifth, nor the Archangels of the sixth, nor the Christs of the Seventh, but the Logos Itself, Whose Divine Spark it is by which he lives.

Through the intermediation of these hierarchies all rise to the consciousness of the Cosmos, but they never pause or achieve finality upon any plane of the manifested universe, for there is no finality in manifestation.

The first plane is the only plane upon which the Initiation of the Logos is given, but it is this Initiation of the Logos which marks the transition from the involutionary to the evolutionary arc, for it wakens the Divine Spark which has well and truly been called the 'God within.'

and which evolves into union with the 'God without'.

On the evolutionary arc, as he goes up the planes, man no longer looks straight to the Logos, but to his immediate hierarchical superiors; but on the involutionary arc he neither looks back to the Logos, nor on towards matter, but across the diameter of the plane to his gods who are the evolved Entities who are withdrawing from materialization, and in their withdrawal have reached the plane to which he has advanced.

Therefore it is that the primitive religions are along polytheistic lines. Monotheism marks the nadir of materiality and the transition from the involutionary to the evolutionary arc. The Jews, who first achieved this, are the most materialistic of all peoples.

On the evolutionary arc the religions are not polytheistic for, having passed the nadir, entities of this evolution have known the One God. They are, instead, obedient to the hierarchies, for that Light, which when dimmed by the veil of matter is bearable, would be unbearable when matter no longer shelters.

Therefore, upon the subtler planes when consciousness is freed from the brain we never approach the Creator direct but always through those intermediaries who transmit and translate the force from plane to plane, of whom the Group Mind or Ray Exemplar of our evolution is the ultimate.

This teaching, you will perceive, embraces the symbolism of the Caduceus. You see the direct path from the base to the Crown, and you see that the paths wind from side to side of each plane as the downflowing tide of life is made conscious of the higher aspect dwelling upon its plane, and the upgoing tide has to become aware of, and minister to, the downflowing.

The Ray Exemplar presiding over each evolution is a Lord of Mind, and as he is of the third evolution he will have the aspects of the earlier evolutions in his nature. Therefore, while three is the prime symbol of this evolution because its Christ is three-aspected, four is the ultimate symbol. The Trinitarian aspect is the basic, but the Tetragrammatonic is the completion. This is the clue to much.

Remember never to seek to explain anything in manifestion or out of it in terms of the static, for all is kinetic.

# 21.

# The Lords of the First Three Swarms and Natural Laws

Influences simultaneously acting on a planet fall into two main classes:

1. Those of the involutionary arc.
2. Those of the evolutionary arc.

There will be the influences of complete entities of earlier evolutions. These are of the three types already known to you—the Lords of Flame, of Form and of Mind. These function in their spheres as Regents.

The Lords of Flame are the lives behind the natural forces referred to below, and the controllers thereof. The Elements of inanimate nature are their children created by the conceptual action of their intellects in the same way that the Logoidal Mind projects the manifested universe. A Lord of Flame conceives a function, and, having himself evolved beyond the point at which he can develop further by this functioning, withdraws to a higher plane and projects the concepts of that functioning to maintain the function.

Those thought-forms by experience develop a Personality but have not yet arrived at the Individuality, therefore they are spoken of as 'soul-less'.

You will observe that the Divine Sparks develop first a nascent Individuality and then a Personality. But the 'creations of the created' develop first a Personality and then aspire to Individuality. Therefore are they spoken of as 'evil spirits', 'familiars', 'demons' and 'genii'. They are not deliberately malevolent but are incapable of response to aught but the lower aspects. When approached upon their own plane their sole link with the Divine is through the consciousness of their creator. Therefore it is that those who would deal with them need to come with the authority of their respective originators, for then they are approached from their divine aspect, and the reflected Divinity within them responds; otherwise they are approached from the demoniacal aspect and in their lower aspect they respond. These, the servants of the gods, maintain the co-ordinated rhythms of inanimate nature. They are the controlling forces of heat and light, of gravity and of all dynamic reactions.

The Lords of this evolution (the 'creators of the created') rule upon the seventh and sixth planes as Regents of the Elements, or 'Lords of the Elements' as sometimes called, and according to the operation of their nature are the kinetic conditions of the manifested universe, and subject to those, man must perform the actions of his evolution. To these Lords man must give unquestioning obedience, reverence to their greatness, and the gratitude which is due to those who, taking thought, sustain the conditions of his being.

To their servants, or thought-forms—the Elementals—he owes the gratitude due to those who, by their nature, serve but who serve unintelligently. Should he seek to approach them, he does so through the corresponding aspects of his own etheric double, but does so at his peril, for though they will first vivify those aspects they will subsequently absorb them.

Now be it known that these Elementals are evolving upwards, grade by grade through the Personality towards Individuality, and in the event of man making contact with them, some among them might fall to the temptation of black magic whereby evolution is illegitimately hastened, and seek to appropriate an already developed Individuality, and thereby establish their contact with the Divine.

In such an occurrence the opposite to the ordinary form of obsession occurs—the Personality is thrust out and an Elemental consciousness takes it place, and of such it may be said that they have a stone of the earth, or a wave of the sea, or a wind of heaven, or a flame of fire for a heart, for human heart they have not; and because of the strength of the Elements they call unto the Elemental in mankind with a profound calling, and such have always troubled the sons and daughters of man. For they come as beings of a strange and Elemental power that knows not the bonds that bind humanity, and they may be known by these things—they ever seek their own kingdom and sorrow for it (for humanity to them is a crucifixion) and they ever call to the corresponding aspects of men and women, and those who answer they destroy, for they are too strong for them.

It may also happen that one who has made contact with the Elementals, instead of being obsessed may be mated. Then will the Elemental aspect of his nature be linked to an Elemental and yearn towards that unseen lover who is not of human kind. Then there is sorrow for such, for they thirst with a thirst which cannot be slaked within the flesh; and to meet their lovers they must issue forth in the etheric form. Much might be said on this subject.

Should a human being, however, seek contact with the Lords of the Elementals he must purify those aspects of his nature which correspond to their kingdom until they become the refined essence of their qualities. In the stability of earth he is stable. In the mobility of the water he is mobile. In the speed of the wind he is swift and aspiring. In the brightness of the flame he is zealous. Then, being lord of these things within himself he himself is a Lord of the Elements in the microcosm, and may thereby claim kinship with the Lords of the Elements of the macrocosm and the Messengers of the Elements are his servants. There is no other way than this. Those who use the Names without the Power invoke to their own destruction.

The Lords of Form govern all physical and chemical affinities, and to them applies all that has been said of the previous evolution; by their aid we may penetrate into the knowledge of the atomic and chemical laws and relationship of things, for 'Form' is but a co-ordinated relationship.

The interaction between the Lords of Flame and the Lords of Form is very important, for the Lords of Flame are the givers of Life, and the Lords of Form are the merciful givers of Death. It is from the Lords of Form that we learn the laws of Death—the laws of escape and freedom.

To master the forces of Flame we invoke the powers of the Lords of Form.

To master the powers of Form we invoke the powers of the Lords of Mind.

The Lords of Form are the Lords of friction; they enable force to function by confining it, but by friction they disperse it. Therefore are the Lords of Form the Lords of Death, for they bring all things living to an end, and all things kinetic to a standstill; but they make actual that which was potential. They are the Educators. Discipline is theirs though 'punishment' rests with the Lords of Mind.

The Elementals of the Lords of Form determine the nature of all chemical elements, combinations and reactions.

The Lords of Flame are behind the laws of physics.

The Lords of Form are behind the laws of chemistry.

The Lords of Mind are behind the laws of biology.*
The Lords of Humanity will be behind the laws of sociology.

* *Editor's note*: The influences of the Third Swarm through the laws of biology are not dealt with, but it is not difficult for the reader to work them out for himself on the lines corresponding to the elaboration of the influences of the First and Second Swarms.

# 22.

# Influences Which Humanity Exerts Upon Itself

It is not proposed in this teaching to recapitulate known facts in evolution, but rather to supplement that knowledge by the revelation of largely unknown factors, and the explanation of the implications of little-known or misunderstood factors.

In previous lectures we have dealt with pre-human evolutions and their influence upon humanity. In the present lecture we will deal with certain little-known influences which humanity exerts upon itself.

In considering the question of other evolutions occupying the same planet it must not be forgotten that if consciousness be raised above the physical plane to function in another state it is thereby lifted from the sphere of the Earth and comes under the Regency of the Planetary Being corresponding to the plane on which it functions. (This is a matter to be remembered in casting the horoscopes of psychics.)

In this teaching, however, we will deal only with those influences operating on the Earth Sphere. These include those which function on the etheric sub-planes while approaching on the involutionary arc, and those which also influence the Earth on the evolutionary arc.

In the ordinary way, for the creatures of an evolution to look back to the conditions of a phase which they have outgrown is retrogression and to be deprecated. Those who have immediately passed beyond the Earth's sphere are not permitted to look back lest they become earth-bound; hence the evil of interference with the spirits of the recently dead, save for the purposes of giving quittance.

There exists, however, a peculiar modification of evolution whose effects are known to you under the general term of the 'Work of the Great White Lodge' or 'Work of the "Masters"'.

In the ordinary course of evolution the wood grows with the growth of the trees. That is to say that the perfecting of the individual souls perfects the group life. But with the coming in of self-consciousness comes a modification of group life, and certain souls choose the path of the redeemer rather than the path of redemption. They elect to forego the fruits of their efforts and their good karma is added to the racial karma for its modification.

Do not let it be forgotten that all evolution has a sequence in time—or, technically, a sequence in cause and effect, and though the path of evolution be so broad that many are contemporaries, yet the evolutionary types have a well marked sequence. The average of the present humanity may be looked upon as being two-thirds of the way round the cycle, and it should also be remembered, with regard to the individual, that just as all the latencies of the past are innate in him, so are all the potentialities of the future, and that some of these potentialities are on the threshold of actuality.

The full range of the possibilities of the human evolution thus falls into three sections—the latencies, the actualities and the potentialities.

The doctrine of the 'Group-Soul' is closely interwoven with that of the Planetary Being, for as has been previously shown, the Planetary Being is the Personality of the planet, built up out of its experiences derived from the consciousnesses functioning within its sphere.

No consideration of group or individual psychology can be adequate unless allowance be made for the influence of the Planetary Being. This is sometimes referred to as the 'Earth-pull', and as it was built up in the past and contains nothing of the future, it is necessarily purely atavistic, and therefore, relatively speaking, evil.

In contradistinction to the Planetary Being it must not be forgotten that there is the Planetary Entity. This is the Logoidal realization of the existence of a planetary sphere, and the Logoidal concept of its mission and evolution. This corresponds to the Individuality, and development of both aspects takes place till they meet.

With regard to a Planetary Being, however, it is built up out of the realization of the conscious life of its sphere, and as it is not possible to realize a thing until after its occurrence the Planetary Being is always a stage behind humanity in its evolution.

It will be seen that each phase of experience of a developing humanity lays down a corresponding level of Planetary consciousness. This is a reflection, or projection, of evolutionary consciousness, and like all reflections it is reversed, so that the lowest aspect appears on the surface and the highest is concealed in the depths. This is borne out by experience for when we touch the Earth Soul we touch its most primitive aspects first, and it is not until we have penetrated deeply into its sphere that we realize of what it is capable.

It is very necessary in approaching these matters that we should not investigate them until full self-consciousness has been attained. If we approach them by means of sub-consciousness, we make ourselves one with them, and the lesser is under the dominion of the greater—the individual of the mass.

The Planetary Being may be conceived of as having the mass karma of the Earth, and all life on the Earth must be lived in relation to that karma for it makes the mental atmosphere in which we live and move and have our being.

In considering the horoscope, insufficient attention is usually given to the phases of the physical plane—to the changing tides of the Earth and of the Moon. It is not enough to note the Moon's position. It should be observed whether she is in her negative or positive phase. Likewise with the Earth, the seasons of the Elements should be observed. All these play an important part in human affairs for, though they are not determining, they are conditioning.

The past, or biological consciousness, then, lives in the Earth karma and also lives in each individual entity; and the reaction between the individual and the collective atavistic strata is very important.

Wherever the development of a particular aspect has had its seat or 'form,' that aspect will dominate the atmosphere of the locality. For instance, where the Druidical cults built up their powers these powers will remain in evidence and will stimulate that aspect of an individual which they were designed to bring into function; and while this method of bathing in the mental atmosphere is valuable for adjusting the balance of the individual who is lacking in this respect it is injudicious for those who already have an overplus of it; these feel themselves to be alien in the modern civilization and are irresistibly attracted toward the ancient cultures and an oversetting of balance may be the consequence.

Each race maintains its cultural traditions, and each cult survives until the faculties which it was designed to initiate have become the normal inheritance of the species. Then it ceases to be esoteric and becomes exoteric.

Cults do not die because they are cut off from the march of progress but because their spiritual principle is absorbed completely in the life of the race. That which they set out to teach is taken for granted and their duty of teaching is over because the pupil knows the lesson. That which is sloughed off is but the effete accretions of human opinion seeking to explain that which transcends it. But as long as there are souls that require the discipline the cult lives on. The cults of the past gained their power by contacting the strata of the Earth Soul to which their Initiations belong.

Now be it known that these strata have close connection with the Elementals, being used by them for the building of the thought-forms which enable them to assume a species of incarnation. Therefore the contacts of an atavistic cult may be far-reaching.

These things have their place in the armoury of spiritual weapons, but are to be approached with caution for they are two-edged. A knowledge of them is necessary in the study of psychical pathology, but not for self-development. These faculties are normal in us and receive an undue stimulus if unduly fostered.

To each man his own master. Do not select a master of a lower or a different type of evolution.

# 23.

# The Law of Action and Reaction

Action and reaction are equal and opposite. The equivalence of the reaction renders it calculable if the ratio of the transmission be known.

There are seven sub-planes in a plane, seven planes in a Universe of the Seventh Cosmic Plane, and seven planes in the Cosmos. Transmission takes place by sub-planes.

The potency of each sub-plane is the square of the potency of the sub-plane below it. This, you will see, is explained by the fact that the two opposing and equally balanced forces set up a vortex which is the primal atom. When these two forces meet they neutralize each other and the result is a centre of stability which is devoid of force save in its subjective aspects. It may be noted that a static force is the subjective aspect of a force.

If therefore you should be able to separate the gyrating currents which form a primal atom you would have two potencies which would be the equivalent of the latency of that atom. So that instead of one actual latency you have two potencies. So that the atom has been multiplied by itself and transferred from one plane of manifestation to another; and whenever a thing is thus multiplied it is translated to another dimension.

When, therefore, action and reaction are said to be equal and opposite, it must be remembered that they are so in the ordinary sense in which this term is employed, and on the plane under consideration only.

If, however, such conditions should occur that the force should be transmuted from a lower to a higher plane, then the reaction is in the equivalent potency of that plane. Hence it is that when you sublimate a force you square it. When you degrade a force you reduce it to its square root. The term 'degradation' is here employed in its technical sense as the opposite of sublimation, meaning descent into matter.

On the involutionary arc degradation was the means of development.

Hence it is that in the course of Initiatory experiences in which the Soul recapitulates evolution it has to know its depths.

Each atom of matter contains the fruits of an involution. Therefore you will see that if you could completely disintegrate the atoms of matter in an ounce of clay you could shatter the globe on which you stand, but before you could perform that magical process you would have, by the power of your will, to dissolve the cohesion of the Cosmos. Therefore it is not to be anticipated that this experiment will be successfully executed in the immediate future!

Each Divine Spark, by the time it has reached the nadir of involution and is ready to embark upon the path of evolution whereon it is seen to be characteristically human, possesses potentialities which you little realize.

When subjective consciousness is raised from the plane of its habitual functioning to the next superior plane it conforms to the law already enunciated and an inertia is converted into two kineticisms. It is seldom that the consciousness-centres of the lower plane are able to carry this force if the conversion is sudden and total. Hence the saying 'Thou canst not look upon My face and live.' Hence also the fact that where a lesser or more partial form of conversion takes place it is apprehended simply as a blinding flash of light, and when such conversion takes place in its normal form it is performed by the method of addition instead of multiplication.

That is to say, when transmutation is performed from one plane to another by the process of squaring, the result may be described in the words of Scripture 'He walked with God and was not.' When the process takes the form of a many-times repeated multiplication you have the ordinary course of the Path, each grade of Initiation being multiplication. But when you have the process as an addition you have the normal course of evolution.

Each grade of Initiation can be conceived of as a blinding flash of light, and by means of this flash the image of the sub-plane to which it belongs is photographed on the sub-consciousness, whence consciousness reads it at its leisure.

If power be raised a plane you must have a group to receive it. The form for a force raised from one plane to another is built up of the group mind. If a force is raised a second plane, you must have a second grade in your group. You therefore get a grade for each plane.

If, on the other hand, force be degraded a plane, or a sub-plane, an entirely different process occurs. The force being rendered inert, the vehicle through which it functions is an empty channel, standing open; anything may fill it. This is the key to much; it explains obsession.

Now remember that the term obsession is popularly used inaccurately, when what is technically called 'overshadowing' is meant. Overshadowing is a controlling influence exercised by one entity over another. Obsession takes place only when the Soul has been precipitated by the process of the degradation of consciousness. The term 'precipitation' is used because the analogy is exact.

When therefore a true case of obsession has to be dealt with, it is necessary not only to cast out the invading entity but to sublimate the soul. You will see a reference to this in the story of the man from whom the devil was cast out and into whom the seven devils entered finding the house empty.

The degradation of the soul takes place through the operations of the lower types of evolution with which contacts have been formed; it does not take place as a result of a deliberate act of will, but rather as a result of an inhibition of will. Therefore when you are dealing with a case in which the will functions from the inhibiting aspect rather than the kinetic aspect, you must always take care lest such a pull downwards is set up. The inhibited will is more dangerous than the perverted will, because it exposes its possessor to the influence of extra-human forces.

You will see, then, that the occult significance of the maxim that action and reaction are equal has two implications—action and reaction are equal only on one plane but when the functionings of seven planes are considered they are anything but equal, and when an action occurring on one plane has its reaction on another plane the result is a transmutation of values. These values have already been explained to you.

It will no doubt have occurred to you that when a force, being transmuted from one plane to another, exerts its influence on the second plane and withdraws its influence from the first, an alteration of equilibrium will result. This is indeed the case, and it is therefore necessary for the Adept who performs this operation to maintain the adequate equilibrium of stresses. For this purpose he must know the method of properly degrading an equivalent force. This is an exceedingly important point in practical occultism, and concerns the utilization of reverse aspects in their proper compensating potencies.

The Sephiroth when reversed are the Qliphoth. Therein is the key to much, and therefore it is that in every magical operation in which great spiritual potencies are invoked, lesser entities are also employed in their proper aspects, and when what you would term a 'Master' wishes to operate on the physical plane, he will of necessity employ an entity of a lower grade of evolution than his own, and he will be compelled to work through the Personality of that person. In order to restore the equilibrium which he is about to displace, he will then, metaphorically speaking, employ that entity as the nadir of his arc. The force he transmits will be received by the highest aspect of that entity and will be expressed by the lowest and most concrete aspect of the Individuality of that entity, and the Personality will be used for the return flow from the physical plane.

This would be expressed in diagrammatic form by the letter Y of which the two arms should represent the Individuality and Personality and the basal portion the channel of outflowing and inflowing on the physical plane. Upon the Y superimpose an X and you will get the symbol of the outflowing and inflowing forces, the X being formed of two C's back to back—the left-hand being marked with an arrow of outflowing, and the right-hand with an arrow of inflowing.

You will now perceive why continence is often demanded when operations of practical magic are in progress. The return flow having to take place through the Personality in its lowest and most primitive aspect, that aspect has to be upturned so that the force of its expression may return to God Who gave it.

This is but another way of expressing the use of sublimation for the purpose of generating force in the upper planes. The pupil who receives force from his Master on a higher plane for the purpose of transmission to the physical plane must be prepared to effect the transmutation of the corresponding amount of force in his own nature from a lower plane to a higher in order to preserve the necessary balance. It is the neglect of this operation which causes the all too frequent overweighting of the lower aspects of the occultist.

# 24.

# The Law of Limitation – Part I

Limitation is the first law of manifestation, therefore it is the first law of power. This is not sufficiently appreciated. Many people believe that a spiritual power is infinite, which is far from being the case. For the Logos to manifest It has to circumscribe Itself. But a spiritual power is so much greater than the potencies of the lower planes that when brought to bear upon them it overcomes all resistances.

In order to bring any energy into manifestation it is necessary to provide it with a form or vehicle. The form is built into the substance of the plane immediately superior to that upon which it is desired to produce an effect, and through this channel is directed the force it is desired to invoke. To invoke a force without directing it is to disperse it. It is only by a knowledge and utilization of the Law of Limitation that power can be conserved.

In order to achieve an end you must outline that end and limit yourself to it, rejecting all that is irrelevant; and note this point—the first process in the invocation of power is the rejection of that which is irrelevant. This is another name for concentration. The Law of Limitation means the concentration of power by the rejection of the irrelevant. This is not sufficiently understood.

In all undertakings the prime requisite for success is to know what you cannot do. This is discrimination. The Law of Limitation is the necessary corollary of the laws governing the invocation of power.

When it is desired to put through an enterprise, first proceed to think the matter out in all details, clearly outlining the end it is designed to achieve. Next consider the means whereby that end may be achieved. Next proceed to eliminate all desire for anything unconnected with that aim—this is a most important detail. In other words you render yourself one-pointed.

It may well be that in doing this you put aside certain legitimate human aims. Put them aside with a proviso that in due season their claims will be considered, and then proceed with utter ruthlessness to limit yourself to the matter in hand so that you have but one desire and all else is subordinate to it. Think of nothing else, dream of nothing else, until the matter is finished. Then, having achieved this complete circumscription of desire and limitation of the content of consciousness, invoke the power for its performance, and in a flash the thing will be done. Thorough preparation means quick completion. In these matters insufficient time is usually given to the preparation, and therefore the achievement is incomplete.

If it is your intention to invoke spiritual potencies you must prepare for them by the complete dedication of the content of consciousness. It must not be forgotten, however, that such a narrowing of consciousness would destroy the balance of the nature if persisted in unduly. Therefore learn to alternate periods of concentration with periods of expansion into fullness of life, so that the broadened consciousness and developed character act as a background for the intensification and limitation of desire which brings spiritual potencies into manifestation on the physical plane. It is the lack of this proportion which leads to fanaticism and loss of balance.

It is by the limitation of the content of consciousness that you achieve the concentration of power. But it is by the development and expansion of consciousness that you achieve the basis of limitation; because limitation implies discrimination, and a limitation of consciousness is entirely different from a limited consciousness. Limited consciousness implies the exclusion of experience. Limitation of consciousness implies selection of experience and the focussing of attention upon the chosen subject. It is the Law of Limitation which is implied in the power to focus. It is by availing ourselves of resistances that we are able to obtain a purchase upon diffused manifestation.

The greater part of the resistance experienced by the neophyte in his attempt to practise the occult arts is the resistance of inertia. In order to set in motion that which is inert it is necessary for the Ego to obtain a purchase upon a similar resistance. Inertia is then balanced against inertia, and the kineticism of the Ego avails to turn the balance. In this way results may be achieved that the unaided will could not obtain.

It is necessary that those in the service of the Hierarchy should acquire a knowledge of the 'magical' arts, because these enable you to invoke and concentrate power effectively. It is the use of these arts for evil ends which is forbidden, but the use of them under the law is an economy of energy.

Remember, then, that in all undertakings, limitation is the secret of power. This does not imply, however, that you should always seek to achieve small things. Always correlate your effort with the Cosmos itself, and see your work in relation to the whole, but rigidly circumscribe the section of that Cosmic whole which you take into your hands. To weigh yourself in the scale against that which is greater than yourself is to be outweighed by the inertia of the mass but to circumscribe a section of the mass, and separate it from the whole is to enable yourself to achieve piecemeal that which you cannot achieve in bulk.

In making this circumscription, look for the natural lines of cleavage, seek the joints of the problem. In all affairs there will always be points where matters can be segregated, and other points that will resist partition. Look for these on the astral plane, among the emotions involved in the matter. The scheme as a whole may be envisaged as one on the mental plane, but upon the astral plane the lines of cleavage may be seen. The object of immediate desire may be distinguished from the object of remote desire. The object which is desired by one aspect of a complex nature may be distinguished from the object which is desired by another aspect. If you yourself circumscribe consciousness to a single point it will be brought to such a fine edge that it can be inserted along the lines of cleavage of an uncircumscribed enterprise and deal with that enterprise piecemeal.

It is the focus of consciousness which enables power to brought to bear and work to be accomplished with that power, but it is the extension of consciousness that provides the necessary base upon which that force obtains a purchase. The concentration at the apex must be supplemented by breadth at the base. This is a point which is often forgotten.

# 25.

# The Law of Limitation — Part II

The Law of Limitation is the basis of occult practice. It is the secret of power, therefore it was withheld from those on the probationary path. They were taught of the existence of an infinite reservoir of power, and to meditate thereon. They were taught to meditate on the formless power. This enabled the power to use them, not them to use the power.

But when the knowledge is acquired of the method of channel-building through the lower planes, it is possible to direct power to any given end. When this is accomplished power is translated from the planes of the Individuality to the planes of the Personality; not within the organism, but without. It is therefore necessary to have the knowledge of the method of making forms. 'As above, so below'.

When the Unmanifest willed to become manifest motion flowed in a circle returning whence it originated. To make a form upon the concrete mental plane, thought must move in a circle, returning whence it originated. Starting with a concept, it must proceed logically from that concept, reasoning from the general to the particular upon the outgoing arc, and from the particular to the general on the arc of returning, thus envisaging both sides of the question and correlating them. This is the first stage.

The concept thus formed should then be transferred to the realm of feeling. This corresponds to the Ring-Pass-Not.

The concept should then be subjected to the driving force of the nature. This corresponds to the Ring-Chaos.

Now the Ring-Cosmos is the concept on the mental plane, the Ring-Chaos is the driving force of the instincts, and the Ring-Pass-Not corresponds to the Upper Astral aspect. By meditating on these correspondences you will learn much. This is your archetypal form, and within it will be built up all the actions and reactions arising in relation to the matter in hand, but this matter must always first be circumscribed by the clear definition of consciousness. The second reaction of consciousness arises with regard to the desires relating thereto, and the third aspect concerns the use of the primitive forces for the generation of power.

The Cosmic aspect of the concept having thus been set up, manifestation in the world of form takes place within the circumscribed sphere. Without this circumscription there is no manifestation.

The prime law of the involutionary arc is the Law of Limitation.

The prime law of the evolutionary arc is the Law of the Seven Deaths.

The Law of Limitation has for its basis the Law of Action and Reaction.

The Law of Action and Reaction has for its basis the phenomena connected with the curve. The curve sufficiently prolonged becomes a circle. A segment of a curve is an arc. The pendulum is the type of action and reaction, equal and opposite. Prolong the arc described by the pendulum and you will form a circle, of which the length of the pendulum is the radius. This explains much in relation to the transmutation of force from plane to plane.

Incarnation is based upon the Law of Limitation; Karma, on the Law of Action and Reaction, and because it is only in a limited sphere that equal and opposite action and reaction can take place, 'force' has to be manifested as 'form' so that the fruits of its action may be returned again to the sphere whence it originated.

The building of a vehicle for incarnation follows the lines already laid down. Again we have the circumscribing which delimits the matter to be worked out in that incarnation. Each soul determines its own matter. The Oversoul therefore is the Lord of Karma to each one. It is this you invoke in all matters connected with your fate. You invoke your own Essential Self.

The Law of Limitation is analogous to the mathematical concept concerning measurements of surfaces, it has a two-dimensional aspect. It is by the introduction of a third dimension that we transcend the Law of Limitation, and man, having a consciousness of three dimensions, can use the Law of Limitation by transcending it. Upon whatever plane the Law of Limitation acts it can always be transcended by the addition of a dimension to consciousness. This is the secret of the control of the Law of Limitation.

The Law of Limitation gives the means of calculating the conditions under which an operation has to be carried out. If you do but determine these conditions you are controlled by these conditions, but if you can raise consciousness to the plane which can perceive them as a synthesis;

if you can perceive the abstraction which comprises them, and can then delimit that abstraction, and consider it in relationship to the condition of its plane apart from the Law of Limitation; if you can conceive it in relation to the Cosmos, having in conception linked that idea to the Cosmos by envisaging the relationship between the whole and the part, it is then possible for consciousness, bearing this Cosmic idea in mind, to be redirected to the finite aspect of that idea, and then to approach it from another and superior dimension; and, while utilizing the Law of Limitation to circumscribe the matter in hand, to transcend these limitations.

This method can be applied, not only to the handling of any matter or affair, but also to the building of the bodies in an incarnation, and to the handling of karma during incarnation, for do we but once see our predestined fate in its relationship to Cosmic law we have mastered our fate. The Essential Self always sees it thus, because the Essential Self has a Cosmic relationship by means of the Logoidal imprints on the Divine Sparks; but the Lower Self, having a terrestrial relationship, sees all things in relation to 'birth' and 'death', 'beginning' and 'ending'.

So long as consciousness dwells in the senses it will view things from the standpoint of the senses, of 'pain' and 'pleasure', 'beginning' and 'ending'. But when it is raised to the relation of Cosmic things, it will see all things in relation to evolution—to the curve that comes round the whole circle, not to the straight line of the partition of finiteness.

The Personality is what it is by virtue of the Law of Limitation, the Individuality is what it is by virtue of the Law of the Nature of the Cosmos; and the ladder from the Personality to the Individuality has seven rungs, and these rungs are the 'Seven Deaths', for it is the Law of Limitation that brings to birth, but it is the Law of Death that brings to life. For birth is death, and death is birth. All are born 'blind', which mercifully prevents them from knowing that they are dead. You do not realize that your plane is the plane of death, and that our plane* is the plane of life. Those who are in matter are in the grave, they are dead and buried. Death and Initiation produce the same results, therefore it is that all Initiations contain the symbolism of death and burial.

Always remember that upon the material plane death and loss mean freedom and resurrection. Possessions are as the earth that is heaped upon the corpse. Learn, therefore, to look down upon your dead bodies

* The plane of the Communicator.

and to galvanize them with your life, but do not make the mistake of living in them.

It is very useful to be able to project consciousness on to the mundane sphere, but it is very disadvantageous to be fettered by the conditions of that sphere. You are held to that sphere by two things—fear and desire.

Initiation will enable you to live upon our* plane, though still attached to brain consciousness. It is therefore that the Degrees* teach: First, the overcoming of desire; secondly, the overcoming of fear; and thirdly, death and resurrection.

By knowing the Law of Limitation and transcending it you can use it. Having circumscribed the task you have set yourself, see it in relation to the Cosmos. By seeing the Cosmic Archetype you will draw in the force of that ideal; and by seeing the circumscribed form which it is desired to manifest, you will focus that force.

* Degrees = Stages of directed progress; it is a term used in the traditional methods of climbing the 'ladder of seven rungs'.

# 26.

# The Law of the Seven Deaths

Learn now the implications of death.

**The First Death**

As has been previously recorded, when two lines of movement intersect a vortex is set up. These two lines of movement then neutralize each other so that they cease to exist as movement and become a centre of stability. This is the First Death.

**The Second Death**

Action and reaction are equal and opposite upon the plane of their inception. They act, react, and continue to manifest in cyclic form. But when transmuted from one plane to another, they cease to manifest upon the first plane, and come into being in a different form upon the next plane. If this translation be viewed from the plane of the inception of these forces it is called death. If it be viewed from the plane of the reception of these forces it is called birth.

If an evolutionary change be viewed from the more primitive aspect it is looked upon as death. If it is viewed from the more evolved aspect it is looked upon as birth. This birth is the Second Death.

Let us make this clear by an example. Life, having evolved beyond the capacity of lowly forms to give it expression, builds itself higher forms. The fossilized remains of the abandoned lower forms are found among the débris of life. They have undergone death; their race is extinct; they are no more; but the life has achieved rebirth into a higher type of vehicle. It is only by the abandonment of the simpler form that life can enter the more complex, though the consciousness that is in the plane of the simpler form sees therein a tragedy because it cannot conceive the higher life and it sees its own passing prefigured; but the consciousness which is of the higher life sees the birth of a new manifestation and rejoices, for it sees the fuller expression of its potentialities.

**The Third Death**

Each individualized consciousness lives to die and dies to live. It is only by death that we can reap the fruits of life. We graze in the fields of Earth, and we lie down in the fields of Heaven to chew the cud. It has been said 'for one hour's study do three hours' meditation'. In death is the soul's meditation and in life its study.

Did you only 'live', all experiences would pass through consciousness and leave but little impression after the first few pictures had filled all available space. All would be concrete, unrelated, unsynthesized; in the meditation which is 'death', the abstract essence of life is extracted, and instead of a million concrete images there is the abstract concept. Learn to trust death. Learn to love death. Learn to count upon death in your scheme of things, and regularly perform the exercise of visualizing yourselves as dead and conceiving how you shall then be, for thus you will learn to build the bridge between life and death, so that it shall be trodden with increasing ease. See yourselves as dead and working out your destiny. See yourselves as dead and continuing your work from the plane of the dead. Thus shall the bridge be built that leads beyond the Veil. Let the chasm between the so-called living and the so-called dead be bridged by this method, that men may cease to fear death.

**The Fourth Death**

Four is the 'linking' number. The fourth body being the highest aspect of the Personality links it with the Individuality, and the Fourth Death is called the 'linking' death—the 'teaching' death, or alternatively may be known as 'sleep'. Sleep is a miniature death just as death is the major sleep, and a knowledge of the nature of sleep assists to explain death. The nature of sleep is insufficiently understood. The impressions of sleep received by the waking consciousness are misleading. In sleep the physical plane is dissociated from the other planes, and the soul thus freed receives no longer the impressions coming through the five gates of the senses and we say 'it sleeps and is passive'; but the Individuality wakes and is active. In waking the Individuality sleeps, and in sleeping life the Individuality wakes. This is the rule for the majority; but there comes a time in the evolution of some when the Personality is capable of being used by the Individuality to express itself. This calls for a highly developed Personality and a highly evolved Individuality. The Individuality is referred to in the sacred writings as the 'Angel that ever beholds the face of God'.

During the waking life of the body the Individuality is intent upon translating into its own terms of abstraction the concrete impressions flowing into the lower soul. When it is no longer thus in-turned it becomes objective upon its own plane and beholds the 'face of the Father'. It then measures itself by the Divine standard and makes such adjustments as are within its power; but the adjustments of the spirit are aeonial and are measured by the span of Heaven.

During sleep the little-evolved soul may not, however, sink into oblivion, but, being much concerned with the unsatisfied desires of the flesh, may continue to function in relation to the thought-forms begotten of these desires. It dreams the dreams derived from unsatisfied passions and the urge of the instincts. The Individuality is not freed, and instead of beholding the 'face of the Father which is in Heaven' beholds the reversed image of the human form and thereby develops in its likeness. The Individuality, being unable to function on its own plane, makes no growth and remains unevolved; and the Personality becomes an exaggerated caricature of itself. From this it can be freed only by the Third Death, thereby enabling the Individuality to assert itself, but if the Third Death be incomplete the lower soul will continue to dream upon the astral plane. This leads us to the question of the Fifth Death.

**The Fifth Death**

The death of the Personality. The Personality, when withdrawn by death from the body, yet continues to live and to function as a Personality, and the man is in no wise changed and still 'answers to the name he bore in the flesh'. In the Lower Hells he burns with desire until the possibilities of desire are burnt out. Desire then remains only as an abstract idea and is part of the Individuality. He then dies to the lower desires but continues to live in the higher desires.

These in their turn he learns to be finite and mortal; he finds them to constitute barriers between himself and his Father Whose face he would behold, and he desires to escape from them. He would no longer love with the personal love which loves a person, but with the higher manifestation of love which itself is Love and loves no person or thing but is a state of consciousness in which all is embraced. He then seeks freedom from the lesser love, and it is this desire for release from that which though good is finite in order to realize the good that is infinite which causes the Fifth Death, and he is born into consciousness of the Individuality, and lives upon the plane of the Individuality, perceiving the 'face of his Father Which is in Heaven'.

But with the waking of desire come again the dreams, and with the dreams comes the recall into matter. The Spirit, beholding the face of its Father until consciousness is weary with Its brightness, closes its eyes and sleeps; and sleeping, it dreams of its unfulfilled desires and so it is born again, for upon the plane of desire a state of consciousness is a place, and as we desire, so are we reborn. Thus each man makes his own Karma.

It may be asked, how then is it that men make for themselves suffering and limitations which they could not desire? It is because they reap not the fruits of fantasy, but the fruits of actuality. They are given *the results of that which they have permitted themselves to desire, not the thing they desire.* To exemplify—the man who desired power would obtain vanity. To obtain power he would have to desire the qualities which confer power, namely strength, foresight and wisdom. The man who desires power builds for himself the consciousness of the vain egotist. The man who desires strength, foresight and wisdom, builds for himself the consciousness of power.

**The Sixth Death**

This is trance, in which the body sleeps but the soul is awake. It is active upon its own plane. It may function upon the sphere of its lower aspects, the instincts, with the body as a background: or it may function upon the sphere of its higher aspects—with the concrete mind and the emotions as a background. In normal psychism picture consciousness portrays the events of the inner worlds as in a magic mirror, the conditions of focus being determined by the emotional states.

When psychic consciousness is focussed in the instincts and passions with matter as a background, consciousness is transferred to the etheric matter which is withdrawn from the dense vehicle in order that it may act as the vehicle of passionate desires; then are seen the manifestations of the lower magic, dangerous and evil in all its forms, degrading to the Personality because its life is lived in relation to matter and not to spirit. Live all life with God for a background and measure all your deeds against the span of Heaven and assess them in relation to the Cosmos, so shall your sin seem grievous in your sight and your errors be very small.

**The Seventh Death**

Illumination. In the Seventh Death consciousness is withdrawn from the Personality and made one with the Individuality and then a man ever beholds the face of his Father Which is in Heaven, even when he himself sojourns upon Earth. Thus it is that the illuminated Initiate is not as other men. Complete Initiation is a living death.

Those who desire the things of the senses and the pride of life use the words 'living death' to denote the most terrible fate that can befall man; but those who have knowledge know that the 'living death' means the freedom of the spirit brought through to the plane of matter. It means the consciousness of the 'Abiding Presence' in the midst of the consciousness of the senses. It means awareness of Heaven while dwelling upon Earth. Therefore the Initiate goes to the living death which is freedom whilst still in the body, for death annuls the Law of Limitation, frees the potentialities of the spirit, gives sight to the blind and power to the impotent. That for which we longed vainly in life we realize in death, for death is life and life is death.

To the wider consciousness the womb is a grave and the grave is a womb. The evolving soul, entering upon life, bids farewell to his friends who mourn him, and taking his courage in both hands and facing the great ordeal and submitting to suffering, enters upon life. His first action in life is to draw breath. His second action with that breath is to set up a cry of distress, because he has entered upon the task of life with grief; and his aim in life is to make life bearable. But when he enters the grave he passes through a gateway into the wider life of consciousness; and when the Initiate would pass to the wider life of consciousness, he passes to it through a gateway which symbolizes death; and by his death to the things of desire he obtains freedom, and as one dead he walks among men. In the death in life, which is the freedom of the spirit in the bonds of flesh, he transcends the Law of Limitation; being dead, he is free; being dead he moves with power among those buried in the flesh; and they, seeing the Light shining brightly through him, know that he is dead, for the Light cannot shine through the veil of flesh. While consciousness is incarnate in the body the Light cannot shine through that consciousness; but when consciousness is discarnate the Light shines through it. If the discarnate consciousness is still manipulating its body, then that Light shines through into the world of matter and illuminates men. But remember this, and meditate upon it—the illuminated Initiate is a dead man who manipulates his body that he may thereby serve those who cannot otherwise be approached.

## 27.

# The Law of Impactation

The true method of impactation is but little known because it involves the inner principles of polarity.

Impactation may be defined as the act of bringing a force of a subtler plane through to a denser plane upon the involutionary arc. This must be distinguished from degradation. Degradation is a similar act upon the evolutionary arc. We speak of the degradation and the sublimation of a force upon the evolutionary arc, and of impactation and disintegration upon the involutionary arc. An important concept concerning the dynamic standard of good and evil is contained in this distinction. Impactation then is the act of advancing a force in evolution by developing it upon the 'form' aspect.

You must remember that the stream of evolving life issuing from the Logos has to descend into matter in order to be organized; and having developed 'form' by its confinement in matter, it uses that form as a mould; or more strictly speaking, a framework (for the subtler surrounds the dense); and when the framework of the dense is withdrawn, the subtle maintains the form it assumed because the system of stresses then developed has become a habit.

The act of sublimation is to separate the dense from the subtle but the act of impactation is to lock two tangential forces into a node of the dense. This you will perceive was the method of the creation of the atoms.

The act of impactation is based upon the use of the Laws of the Attraction of the Centre and the Attraction of the Circumference, and the use of polarity; and in all elaborations of the concepts of polarity the Law of Impactation comes into function because polarity gives rise to impactation; impactation depends on polarity wherein union takes place horizontally and fission takes place vertically.

More has been said than you may realize.

# 28.
# The Law of Polarity

It is impossible to consider the Law of Polarity without considering the Laws of Attraction of the Centre and the Attraction of the Circumference, because polarity has its basis in these two laws. It is according to whether the attraction be towards the centre or the circumference that the negative or positive aspects of force are observed.

The attraction towards the centre gives the negative, and the attraction towards the circumference the positive aspect, and it is these two in polarity that produce the circulation of force. You see the prototype of which this is the correspondence in the positive and negative aspects of the Cosmic Days. The symbol of this is contained in the Caduceus of Mercury. There you see the black and white serpents of positive and negative functions twined from side to side of the staff. Taken in its mundane aspect the staff represents the Ray and the black and white serpents the positive and negative aspects of the Life Wave.

There is also another aspect of polarity in regard to group form. The consciousness of a group is an entity of a negative or female type. It requires to be stimulated by a positive force before it can become creative. That which functions on a subtler plane is positive in relation to that which functions on a denser plane. Should a consciousness conceive the aims of a group on a higher plane than that on which the group conceives them, it becomes positive towards that group and thereby can fertilize it. When fertilization of a group occurs each of the individuals of that group becomes pregnant with a new concept and brings creative work to birth upon the physical plane. They will then have conceived that which the group-leader has begotten, and will then be upon the same plane as the leader. Having conceived the same ideal, they will then be of the same polarity as the leader and it will no longer be possible for him to bring a creative stimulus to that group. This will explain to you the process of florescence and quiescence which groups undergo;

periods of quiescence are not of necessity death.

You will observe that throughout all manifested life the co-operation of two factors is essential for all 'form' building. Force, however, works as a unit because its polarity is in the Logos.

# 29.

# The Law of the Attraction of Outer Space

In considering the Law of the Attraction of Outer Space we have first to enquire how it is that the attraction of Outer Space is able to overcome the attraction of the Centre. In order to understand this problem we have to consider certain basic aspects of the universe which have been previously described.

The Logoidal consciousness, having attained equilibrium, has achieved perfection; and, having attained that which it had conceptually realized, propounds a further conception and seeks its realization.

These formal concepts already conceived within the Logoidal consciousness are continued into more complex syntheses (thereby partaking of the nature of successively developed phases of manifestation), or, to express the same idea in another terminology, passed outward down the planes of manifestation. The growing points of the Logos are projected into manifestation as evolutionary impulses; and the Logos gives the thrust outward which projects the forms, ensouling them with life.

Now it is ever the aim of 'will' to function unconditioned, just as it is ever the tendency of 'form' to condition the unmanifest; and the 'will-to-live' of the Logos, always entering upon the conditioning form, which, as it were, it pushes ahead of itself down the planes, is 'irked' by form; but in the later phases of the Logoidal life unconditioned will is impossible, all action being determined by pre-existing conditions, and the will-to-live of the Logos, which is the life of the manifested universe, has to submit to conditions and be bound in form. Hence the 'warfare between spirit and flesh.'

The will-to-live of the Logos, then, expresses itself through succeeding phases of form until the densest phase is reached. It can no further project the conditioning vehicle of its manifestation, and it strives to free itself from the bondage of form and continue onwards—to employ a metaphor of space—towards those areas of the ether which have not been circumscribed and conditioned by the primal Logoidal Will.

First it is the endeavour of conditioned life to become unconditioned which forms the prime urge—which projects it towards outer space.

Secondly there is the natural tendency towards equilibrium, and of the forces under high pressure within a manifested universe to diffuse themselves into the comparative vacuum of outer space.

Thirdly, there is the picture of the Penumbra—all those moulds which are marred in the making—all those evolutionary concepts which fail in their realization—all misplaced forces and souls that have failed in their task, being rejected by their Individualities—all that in fact which it is desired to reject from the Logoidal consciousness and which not having been disintegrated against the inner shell of the Ring-Pass-Not remains as an image in the reflecting ether of space upon what may be figuratively termed the outer surface of the Ring-Pass-Not (immediately between that and the Ring-Chaos of the universe), and there may be descried.

Any consciousness, then, which ventures to the nether side of matter will discern across the great gulf, which is the Ring-Pass-Not of the universe, the reflected images of all falsified hopes and abortive attempts at manifestation—and these, as it were craving for the force which should bring them into manifestation, call across the gulf to whatever elements are akin to them in that which presents itself at the barrier; and so it is that all evolving force, whether in the universe or in the individual, having penetrated to fundamentals, looks across the great gulf fixed by Cosmic law and sees the simulacra of its hopeless dreams promising fulfilment, and it is tempted to continue forward on that path of outgoing upon which the divine momentum projected it, and, by means of the further momentum acquired by its own motion, to leap that gulf into the freedom of Outer Space where there is no law, and men are as gods.

For when a unit of consciousness is freed from a manifested universe by transcending law (law being consummated in a perfect obedience), it becomes the nucleating centre of a new Logoidal sun; this is the mystery of Godhead. But when a unit of consciousness that has not fulfilled the law escapes it is an unconditioned will; this is the mystery of evil (positive evil), personified as devil. This Temptation of the Nadir comes to all in the course of evolution.

From the Divine upon the outgoing arc life has to penetrate into the fundamentals; and having touched the fundamentals, having attained the summit of its powers, it has to reject the temptation of the desire-image reflected from Outer Space, and retrace its steps in humility back to the source of its life; winning the realization that freedom is attained not by escape from limitations and conditions but by adjusting the balance to a perfect equilibrium.

Equilibrium of conflicting forces being attained, form is stereotyped and can be left to develop the corresponding consciousness, and the ensouling life withdraws to a higher plane, bearing with it the reaction-capacity acquired in the lower plane but no longer bound by the conditions of that plane. This will be dealt with more fully in the succeeding lecture.

The Attraction of Outer Space, then, is the attraction of unconditioned power; it is the temptation to escape from the laws that have built us up and to exercise the powers gained under these laws without the equivalent responsibility. This may be seen exemplified in the life of the man who, enjoying all the advantages of a highly developed culture, brings to them the aims and the ideals of an unevolved state of existence.

The Attraction of Outer Space is the temptation to break away from evolution and the Cosmic law and to function as a god. Such gods are those who are propitiated in the rites of devil-worship.

# 30.

# The Law of the Attraction of the Centre

The law of the Attraction of the Centre contains the secret of the Mystery of Love. It may be considered under three aspects: First in relation to Evolution, secondly in relation to Initiation, and thirdly in relation to Devolution and the Left-hand Path.

**In Relation to Evolution**

When a form of life has attained its utmost complexity in material organization, unification begins. This is obtained by means of the synthesis of principles upon a higher plane and, this having been secured, devolution of the physical form sets in. This marks the transition through the nadir of the Evolutionary Arc.

Let us elaborate this concept. Ideas of life-expression, having been evolved by entities of a higher grade than the life-form under consideration, are projected upon these life-forms in the etheric kingdom as they are approaching materialization, and in the malleable matter of the etheric type they are worked out, and this acts as a framework for the subsequent physical form.

The life-forces, compelled to circulate in the forms built of matter, develop a set of magnetic stresses. These having been developed the material form can be discarded and the system of stresses remains as an etheric mould. Thus does an inceptive idea pass through the plane of manifestation in matter and become a conceptive idea.

There are many different devices employed for obtaining the same result, and, though each of these owes its conception to a different inceptive idea—a different attempt to work out a design—the conceptive idea of perfected action is the same for all. So that that which was multiplicity in its origin, by the perfection of its development arrives at unity.

*One* is the symbol of the First Manifest or the Absolute. Whatever reduces multiplicity to unity—or a 'complex concrete' to a 'simple abstract' is approaching the Centre. The approach to the Centre is not a movement in space, but a unification.

Now note the difference between unification and simplification, because this is the clue to much. Unification is achieved by evolution and simplification is achieved by devolution. Unification is the final synthesis—simplification is the ultimate analysis or return to type. One is advancement to completion, the other a regression to the commencement.

The concept of the Return to the Centre might be considered as an extension of the Centre; for when return to the Centre takes place, the Centre is thereby extended; and we are taught that the Return to the Centre is the goal of evolution. If this idea be meditated upon it will be seen that such a Return to the Centre should involve the extension of the Centre, for if all that is external becomes internal the boundary of the Centre must be extended. In very truth it may be conceived that the Return to the Centre means that the Centre is extended to the circumference and all things are as is the Centre. This implies the spiritualization of all the planes.

Such a concept has two aspects—the 'form' aspect, and the 'force' aspect. Force flows towards the Centre, withdrawing from the circumference. It therefore follows that the Centre, to accommodate it, must flow out. Thus it is that the substance of each plane, having had its native force withdrawn, is recast by the influences of the extending Centre into forms approximate to those which prevail upon the Seventh Plane.

The withdrawing of force marks the end of a Cosmic Day and the beginning of a Cosmic Night. The outflowing of the Centre is the work of the Cosmic Night—and the secrets of the Cosmic Night have never hitherto been revealed.

The outflow of pure spirit over all planes of matter takes place during the Cosmic Night, and all archetypal forms remaining in the vicinity of the magnetic stresses are thereby galvanized, but they have no real life having as yet no reincarnating principle and therefore no memory, and at the end of the Cosmic Night the Spiritual Tides withdraw leaving the field to the emptiness of the Cosmic Dawn. But the forms over which the Cosmic Tide has flowed have been adjusted to Cosmic stresses and therefore all types of evil have been corrected.

This is the cleansing of matter which takes place between each Cosmic Day and neutralizes the forces of inertia; and as the forces of inertia have their roots in the Law of Limitation and the Law of Limitation has its roots in Cosmic Evil, you will see the significance of the work of the Cosmic Night, and you will also see the deeper significance in the words 'The Powers of Darkness'.

It is necessary, if you are to understand the deeper implication of occultism, that you should see that the darkness leads through twilight to dawn, and the day leads through twilight to darkness. 'Good' and 'Evil' may be conceived of as areas of Light and Shadow through which a spinning ring revolves, and 'Evil' has its work to do as well as 'Good'. The God of Light and the God of Darkness are but the actions of the right and left hand of the Father. The right hand gives and the left hand takes away. The right gives that which is to be, and the left takes away that which has been. The right sends out into manifestation and the left beckons back again; but you, looking as in a mirror, call right, left, and left, right.

The Attraction to the Centre takes place up the Path of Returning, and should that attraction set in prematurely it causes the life to flow back to an earlier aspect. This involves a devolution of life before there is a devolution of form. When this returning flow takes place in relation to Life, we see the development of parasitic types of existence. This explains the problem of bacterial disease; other types of life which are saprophytic are not of this Evolution at all, but are functioning under the dominion of the 'Lords of the Dark Face' who are the scavengers of the Gods.

You will perceive from the foregoing that a return to the Centre means a fading of a Day of Manifestation, and as the daylight fades the spiritualizing darkness of the Unmanifest flows over the fields of matter. And this must always be borne in mind in considering this problem, for as the light withdraws from the outward circuit of matter, so the spiritualizing influences begin to flow out from the innermost circuit of Spirit, and this process continues until such time as all light be withdrawn, and the concentric circles of manifestation be completely overflowed by the cleansing Waters of Darkness; but meanwhile there is a transition stage during which the Waters of Darkness (which name is a symbol of spiritual peace, cleansing, and regeneration), make preparation for new life. These Waters, then, are percolating through the planes of manifestation so that the seen will be interpenetrated by the unseen. This brings us to the second aspect of the subject of the Attraction of the Centre—the question of Initiation.

### In Relation to Initiation

Those entities that have returned to the Centre at the conclusion of their evolution flow out again as the forerunners of the Shadow of the Spirit. It is these who are the Initiators. They themselves have been able to progress in advance of evolution by being themselves initiated by developing entities of preceding evolutions according to the planes at which they took Initiation; the Lords of each plane being the completed fruits of the evolution which had its culmination on that plane. These are the Initiators of each evolution until those who are initiated, themselves having passed through the Light, are proceeding outwards again.

By the action of these entities those who are initiated proceed from the surface to the sub-stratum of their plane and it is only when the Waters of Regeneration have penetrated through the cracks and fissures of receptive consciousness of a plane that initiation can take place on that plane. Thus it is that at this stage the Greater Illumination can take place only out of the body, for in this phase of evolution the Waters of Regeneration have not yet reached the physical plane.

### In Relation to Devolution

The Attraction of the Centre has a third aspect in devolution, or the way of the Left-hand Path if applied to consciousness.

In relation to evolution, devolution means the withdrawal of life from any given type of form, and the disintegration of the form. The systems of magnetic stresses which life generated in them are then left as empty shells upon the etheric sub-planes. These shells should await the cleansing of the Waters of Regeneration that flow out in the tides of the Cosmic Night.

It sometimes happens, however, that souls which are sufficiently developed to have reached the point when they feel the Attraction of the Centre upon the Path of Returning, and yet are insufficiently developed in certain aspects to be ready for evolution because they have not yet sufficiently undergone involution, may set out to return to the Centre before they have passed the nadir. They will then be moving through planes from which the life has withdrawn, and whereon lie the empty shells awaiting the coming of the Tides of the Cosmic Night. These souls will then avail themselves of these systems of magnetic stresses of a primitive type for the expression of their functions. This will explain much if meditated upon.

When, however, these souls having outgrown and destroyed the shells (and thereby impeded their subsequent evolution) continue on their devolutionary path, they reach a point when there are no more shells for their ensouling and they will then be unable to maintain form, and will dissolve into the unorganized elements of substance and cease to be potent for Evil or potential for Good. That is the record of the Left-hand Path.

Evolution by the Right-hand Path is accomplished through the withdrawal of the perfected Life from the forms which separate, the synthesis of the principles which the forms were designed to express, the sublimation of the principles into ideals, and the realization of the ideals by the Logoidal Consciousness. Such is the record of evolution upon the Right-hand Path.

It will be seen then that the essence of evolution is unification; and the manifestation of the unificatory principle upon the planes of manifestation is Love. Whether that love be intellectual sympathy on the plane of the concrete mind, or physical unity on the plane of matter, Love in all its aspects is the symbol of the Logos as One.

The aim of evolution is to make all things one, and upon the planes of manifestation there are but two things which make all things one—Death and Love. Death is the manifestation of the Left-hand Path, and Love is the manifestation of the Right-hand Path. Whoso loves, however dim may be his concept of Love, is manifesting a unification, and unification is the goal of Evolution. God is One. Love makes one—therefore it is truly said 'God is Love.'

Whosoever expresses Love, brings Spirit, which is One, into manifestation. To be separate is to be dead. Therefore choose Love and live.

# Addenda

The additional material set out here has the same authority as the body of the work, but was communicated some years after it. While it has in many instances a specific reference to certain chapters it is not here given with that reference to those chapters since it has also a general reference to the teaching as a whole and provides a useful elucidation of the general matter in the book. Generally speaking it refers more to the first twenty chapters of the book than to the later but, of course, the more the book is understood as a whole the more useful will the additional material be.

**1**

Each Cosmic Atom has within itself forces of two Rays which set up the primal vortex though later it went out along the path of one Ray only. The two Ray-forces are the positive and negative factors in the vortex, the negative or latent representing a sort of subconsciousness. Examination of the 'Ray-type' of an individual would call for Sidereal Astrology—a far more complicated and deep astrology than astrology as now practised.

**2**

The Lords of Flame and the Lords of Mind do not meet upon the planes in the progress of the First Three Swarms, but there is a process at a later date whereby a Lord of Flame can as it were fuse with a Lord of Mind, thus becoming to all intents a Lord of Mind. The process is very difficult to describe: there takes place a kind of absorption so to speak, somewhat comparable to the coalescence of an Individuality with a highly developed Personality in a human incarnation, somewhat comparable but not the same. A Lord of Mind who chooses to carry on certain work for a Lord of Flame absorbs the 'experience' of the Lord of Flame somewhat in the manner that an Individuality absorbs the experience of a Personality (but in this case the comparison is reversed since the Lord of Mind corresponds to the Personality absorbing the experience of a Lord of Flame corresponding to the Individuality) and goes forth as a Lord of Mind with the far-off contact (of a Lord of Flame) still working behind him.

Many of the Lords of Flame are what we now call the Archangelic Forces, others guide certain conditions in the universe and have a special contact with the Solar Logos. It is these latter which so to speak steep certain Lords of Mind in their experience and pass their influence into them, thus working through them. The Lords of Flame all have an especially strong Logoidal contact and some were what might be termed sent forth again after the First Swarm had finished its work.

It can be of special benefit to meditate on the Three Primal Swarms because that part of the book which deals with them was set down in a necessarily very approximate manner suited to the 'average intellect'. It is important to bear in mind that all that is said is only an approximation and far more than a merely intellectual appreciation can be gained through meditation on the First Three Swarms.

The material in *The Cosmic Doctrine* is capable of immense expansion—expansion, indeed, beyond the present limits of human understanding.

## 3

To try to put into comprehensible language and yet give something approaching an adequate delineation of the power and majesty of the Three Primal Swarms is a difficult task indeed. The description given in the body of the work conveys little idea of the mighty work undertaken and performed by those Swarms. Those great Waves of Cosmic Life which built the Laws governing the universe, evolution and man are of great importance at all times and especially at the inception of a new Age. Their influence remains behind in man and the universe, and according as man is in touch with these primal beginnings when his own Life-Spark first entered manifestation even so is the type of his Individuality determined. He cannot even now get away from those early stages of development because as his Essential Self took on the influences and reacted to them in the formative stage of his evolution so does each human being at this stage still carry the latent consciousness of those primal actions and reactions. He carries eternally the seed of his own beginning even as the oak carries eternally the acorn within it, and, as the acorn reacted to the soil in which it grew, as it received the air and the sun, in what measure its growth was made and it gradually cast off its outer shell and began to shoot and become an oak tree, so in a sense did man first begin to become man.

As a man reacted to the various planes through which he passed in these primal stages of the Life-Spark—and even then there was a measure, however small, of individual reaction—even so is that man today. As the Spark came down the planes, gathered substance from each plane, and then returned up again he met other Sparks doing the same thing, and so again is it in his life today. In this mass of Sparks on its first descent of the planes there were some which formed a smaller mass within the whole, touching each other more than other Sparks or Groups of Sparks in the whole. Thus did certain special reactions—'friendships' as it were—begin in the primal stages; and in later days of evolution those same Sparks, clothed with matter of all planes passed through, again met those others equally clothed with matter of all planes passed through which had first contacted them in the primal stages. In passing through the planes the matter or substance of each plane was interwoven into the inner vehicles of man and in time built the different forms or vehicles we know now by various names (e.g. the 'Astral Body', 'Mental Body', etc.) and these bodies have also certain subdivisions. The great planetary spheres through which each atom and Divine Spark passed in the course of evolution also had a certain type of influence over it and in a way this is the basis of astrology, though the roots of that study are largely lost and forgotten. Astrology cannot be applied nowadays as the ancient races conceived it because of change among the heavenly bodies, and man himself is changing also.

In his passage down the planes the evolving being came into contact with great planetary Powers which still exercise some control over him—though he may not be aware of it—for he has matter within his make-up which retains a form of contact with those great planetary Powers and their influence on his body, mind, and karma still remains at very primitive levels: for example the Force described as 'The Great Mother' still remains The Great Mother of all living beings and the degree to which a modern man can consciously become aware of this contact is of importance to him.

The great Laws of the Universe were made long before what we call 'man' had evolved sufficiently to come down the planes in the same manner as had come down the great atoms and group-forces which in the beginning built the Universal Powers. The 'Group-Souls' of these latter are behind what we call the great archetypes and with these archetypes esoteric students can be much concerned. And as man eventually returns up the planes at the end of a chain of evolution he reaches on another level his own beginnings. He becomes as it were a god, a type of Logos, in himself at the end of many evolutions gathering together the great chains of experience which will have made himself no longer the individual but in a sense a group from which other units of mind-force emanate. For man begins as a group and individualizes out of the group as evolution goes on and in the end has to return to his own group which is then himself.

Behind that teaching is the 'Collective Principle' or collective sense which, partly or even wrongly understood as it often is, can be found in certain political ideals and systems. This sense has a high ethical basis and strives so to form the character that all should act as one, should act as a team and in a team; for it is the greatest, most intricate and first Divine Law when properly understood. Nevertheless, until the individual be developed to his highest, he cannot be part of the collective unit of Divinity to which he should in the end return. And in each man is that which makes the Trinity—the Three Aspects of the Manifesting Godhead—and these Aspects are in his innermost Spirit as its highest ethic.

When this evolution will have finished, the experience and matter of this plane (Earth) will be garnered up and will pass on to other evolutions in other planets and some of its life-forces will return again in another guise to this planet again. When a man dies portions of his astral and etheric bodies are probably lost for a while to his Individuality, but also they often go to make up certain parts of the new astral and etheric bodies he will have in his new incarnation. That, in a few words, is what has happened all through evolution—the form is broken up and the parts are carried on to build up the form of the next type of life-form; but it is not always known that particles of the denser vehicles—not the physical, but the astral and etheric—the disintegrated astral and etheric bodies of people who have died, go to make up other Personalities. These Personalities may belong later to those Individualities from whose former Personalities the parts come, but it also happens that they may not, and Individualities often have Personalities composed of material which previously has been used in the vehicles of others. This sometimes can account for strange reactions between people in incarnation, so that it is not always necessary to look to meetings in previous lives to explain such reactions. As the human being is in this way so, too, are planets and other heavenly bodies. Planets contain portions of other planets and of other Cosmic times and other evolutions built into their auras, just as this earth is in the aura of the moon* and has contact with many 'lunar particles' of a former evolution. Life in its many-sidedness is not simple by any means, it is woven into a vast pattern which only very advanced Inner Plane Adepti can realize, and there is no pattern that is not in some way linked with all the rest.

**4**

The Planetary Being evolves with the planet and corresponding plane. Its 'bodies'—up to the full complement of seven—and its content of consciousness increased with the arrival and departure of the various Swarms. The activities of the Swarms 4—7 were governed by the 'Lords' of the Three Primary Swarms. Not until a Planetary Being had developed its full complement of 'bodies' could it take a Swarm through the full circuit of evolution, and not until then did the evolution begin of those Sparks which became 'human beings' as we understand the term.

During the descent of the first seven Swarms the influence of the Logos remained paramount in the universe, and any unbalance resulting from the epigenetic activities of the Swarms 4—7 was immediately corrected so that the 'bodies' of the Planetary Beings were not affected.

After the full complement of seven bodies has been acquired by the Planetary Being, however, the influence of the Logos does not fully correct any unbalance because influences from the now fully embodied Planetary Beings intervene. It is at this point that epigenetic factors lay the foundations of individual basic Karma. Each Planetary Being is a stage behind the human evolution proceeding in its sphere, and thus acts as a drag upon it.

**5**

The Three Primary Swarms can be aligned (through the Logos) with the three Cosmic Rings and with the *Essences* of the Four Elements as follows:

* The present moon is not here referred to; the previous moon left behind it substance which goes to make up the aura of the earth. This previous moon left much substance, too, for the present moon, and a great deal of its 'powers' or influences are there, but many, too, of its primitive powers and certain very important factors remain within the earth (in what esoterically is called the 'Inner Earth'), and both these are as well joined into one huge aura which is around both the present moon and the earth.

(1) The Lords of Flame with their great 'stresses of movement' appertain to the Ring Cosmos and to the Element of Fire.

(2) The Lords of Form appertain to the Ring Chaos and to the primal Earth/Water Essence (The Elements of Earth and Water).

(3) The Lords of Mind appertain to the Ring-Pass-Not and to the Element of Air. Individualism can reach a certain limit only and then is turned back on to a higher arc of collectivism. The limits of the human mind are a safeguard of the human race.

**6**

There will come a time when the planetary spheres no longer hold any Swarms passing downards on the arc of involution. When this occurs the condition left behind by the last Swarm will gradually dissolve and for a space nothing will happen. Then there will gradually come in a 'type of vortex' from outside the plane, something that is seeking development, a kind of non-human 'being' which will then go through an involution on a small scale on the empty plane. It will be a very simple kind of life and it will eventually be drawn down to the physical plane; only an experienced student of the subtler sides of esotericism could get any understanding of this form of life—something approaching a new type of Elemental is as adequate a description as any. It should eventually have a connection with a Divine Spark of a much more limited range than the Divine Sparks of the human beings. The subject is a very difficult one to put in words even for approximate ideas: it is, in any case, very remote but has interest.

**7**

The Life-Swarms 4-7 are the common origin of all humanity; in their passage down the planes they have created the great archetypes of humanity and the basic human instincts. They represent a great Group Soul, a collective state from which individual man has gradually emerged. They have made that aspect of the universal Laws which are portrayed in the 'god-forms'. Not until these Laws had become established did man begin to emerge from this group-state, his emergence corresponding with the acquisition by the Planetary Beings of their full complement of bodies—seven in all.

It is this group-state in man that forms the 'collective unconscious' of mankind, the archetypes of which on the *evolutionary* arc (as distinct from the involutionary) man first contacts in dream and vision.

Racial division, therefore, came after this group-state, emergence from which was the beginning of separateness. Community life in its highest sense remains a worthy ideal for its principles seeks to replace separateness with co-operation. These Swarms gradually built what might be called the immediately pre-human shape—even at the time of the fourth Swarm it was still very 'embryonic'. They are of especial interest since on the manner of progression of the Swarms is based the beginnings of what are known as the 'Root Race' types. In these pre-human stages is to be found much of the History of Man, while the gradual formation and development of the Archetypes might be called 'Planetary Embryology'. The human shape as we know it was established by the middle period of the seventh Swarm and the Archetypal forms were due in a sense to the projected concept of the Planetary Being itself which brings through additional concepts of another type than the Logoidal concepts though not necessarily conflicting with those concepts.

**8**

The three 'activities' referred to in Chapter 3 as 'Movement', 'Light' and 'Sound' may be aligned with the three Supernal Sephiroth of the 'Tree of Life'. The numbers assigned to the Sephiroth are connected with the numbers of the corresponding atoms (i.e. of the facets). For example the terrible simplicity of the three-sided atom and the use of three in Binah symbols are obviously related. The four Threes of the Tarot cards have the same basis. Both the 'Tree of Life' and the Tarot will be found to be in line with the tenets of the 'Cosmic Doctrine' if the seeker meditates seriously on the subjects.

**9**

The 'Divine Sparks' and the Great Entity that is the Logos of our system have a common origin in their Prime (Cosmic) Atoms which derive from the Great Unmanifest. These Prime Atoms of a Divine Spark before that Spark comes under the Logoidal influence can be called the 'Seed Atoms'.*

There is a continuity of development from the Prime Atom formed as described in the early chapters to the Divine Spark in each one of us. Just as the Great Entity has evolved from the ten-sided, or travelling,

* This 'Seed Atom' refers to the Cosmos and its difference from the 'seed atom' mentioned at the end of Chapter 12 is plain.

atom of the Cosmos (which itself evolved from the Prime Atom) so have the Divine Sparks evolved from certain of the less complex atoms brought into the wake of the Travelling Atom, or Great Entity, out of whose concepts the Great Entity has created and projected Its universe.

The difference at this point between a Great Entity and a Divine Spark is one of degree but not one of kind for the Great Entity has experience of all the Rays but the Divine Spark has experience of only one Ray—both have experience of all the Planes.

*Certain* of the atoms 'brought over' from the Cosmos to the Universe by the work of the Great Entity became the Travelling Atoms of the Universe. They are not as complex as the Great Entity but are too complex to settle down upon a plane of manifestation and they return to the centre. These atoms 'brought over' by the Great Entity, which become the Divine Sparks are those which in their journeying to the Centre have their 'track in space' impressed with the Logoidal Image and Influence. Thereafter these Divine Sparks became conditioned by the Logoidal Consciousness until the cycle is completed and they became 'freed' from this influence and return to their original nucleus of being as Seed Atoms.

There are, therefore, two ways of considering the Divine Spark. You may look at it from the point of view of the Cosmos or from the point of view of Solar Logoidal evolution: but, in reality the Divine Spark is one thing having its origin in the Unmanifest from which it derives its existence and energy.

The Divine Spark does not derive from the Solar Logos but is conditioned by the evolution of the Solar Logos until the cycle of its Solar development is completed. This takes place when the Individuality, as a result of certain evolutionary processes in the Solar Logoidal jurisdiction comes to the point where it need no longer stay in that jurisdiction but is able to recognize its own true being. At that point it is as though the 'outer' development of the Divine Spark drops away from it and it becomes again purely a seed-atom to which the Individuality thenceforward owes its allegiance. Thus at that stage the Divine Spark, being freed from the *limiting* influences of Solar evolution gives rise to that state of perfect freedom within the Individuality, the state of spaceless and timeless existence—consciousness.

The great responsibility that then devolves upon the Individuality on the 'Right-Hand Path' comes from that Individuality's now established contact with pure and limitless 'energy'. The Individuality is conditioned only by its degree of realization of this contact as it enters on a phase of creative activity; in very truth a god.

Advanced initiations are concerned with the degrees of contact of the Individuality with the *inner* aspect of the Divine Spark (the seed-atom) and the realizations thereof. The cycle of Solar development is governed by the 'Lords of Karma' and it includes the working out of the 'tracks in space' left by the 'karma' when the karma has itself been worked out for the Solar development occurs after the 'track in space' (of the seed-atom) has received the Logoidal Imprint. Thus until the completion of the Solar development the Individuality is not able to bring through pure power without some of the power being diverted to its own needs.

There is, of course, a wide range of gradation between the earlier and later phases but, broadly speaking, the earlier are essentially concerned with the gradual bringing of the Individuality (after preliminary work on the Personality) into contact with its own true being—the seed-atom—whereas the later are the true creative work of those who have achieved in co-operation with their brethren. The preliminary work on the Personality has to be thoroughly carried out before these phases are entered upon.

## 10

The 'inanimate atoms' and the Divine Sparks have a common origin in the Great Unmanifest. They have both been 'brought over' by the Great Entity which is our Solar Logos and from the aggregate of their conceptions of their own images the Great Entity has projected Its universe. Everything that has 'life' in the universe derives that life from its own seed-atom. It is the aim of the Solar evolution to unite eventually the atoms of its universe with their seed-atoms in the Cosmos.

It has been stated that there is a difference of degree but not of kind between the travelling atoms of a universe and that universe's Logos: similarly there is a difference of degree but not of kind between a travelling atom and an inanimate atom.

Only the more evolved of the Cosmic atoms brought over by the Great Entity became travelling atoms in Its universe at the beginning of the Solar evolution and received the Logoidal Impress on their 'tracks in space.' These—not including the First Three Swarms which are different—relate to the human evolution and among them are differences in degree of development caused by factors inherent in their make-up.

The inanimate atoms are less evolved than the travelling atoms and receive the Logoidal Impress during the Solar evolution according to their degree of development because being in and of the Solar universe (their concepts having been used to create it) they are continually being bathed in the Logoidal influences and slowly absorb them. In this way we get the Oversouls of plant and animal life, these Oversouls deriving from the inanimate atoms which are gradually acquiring a Logoidal Impress.

**11**

The basic 'sound' of a human being is implicit in the development of a Divine Spark. The Logoidal Impress can be more accurately conceived of as a sound-vibration than a picture-concept. This idea of primal or basic sound was behind the ancient teachings of number and numerical values. Sound implies rhythm and vibration. That 'Aspect' of the Trinity of the Logos known as the Love-Aspect is the part chiefly at work in the imprinting of the Impress. The higher teaching of the Churches is inspired by this.

**12**

The three Primary Swarms were projected into manifestation each under an impulse from one of the Prime Aspects of the Logos derived from one of the Primary Rings. These Primary Swarms are set apart from the succeeding Swarms and are of a different degree. The Swarms that followed them developed under the influence of the Logos plus the Three Primary Swarms, the Lords of Flame, Form and Mind. They are, therefore, under the influence of the three Cosmic Rings (as were the three Primary Swarms) but also, since the Logos reacts to the Twelve Cosmic Rays, these later Swarms are characterized by the influence of the Rays predominant at the time they received the Logoidal impulse to go forth.

Therefore the great phases of evolution between the sending forth of fresh Swarms are governed by the influences from the Twelve Cosmic Rays. This has reference to the 'Houses' of the Cosmic Zodiac and to the precession of the Equinoxes.

Those who energize these phases and typify them are Ray Exemplars; they stand, so to speak, between the Zodiac and the phases and reflect the Zodiacal influences, acting in a sense as Cosmic mediators. These influences then act upon the Planetary Beings.

**13**

There are two of the ancient god-forms which can be called easily to mind as being readily alignable with the Essential Self, most other god-forms being representative of particular aspects, Cosmic or universal. These two god-forms are Horus and Eros. Of them the former could stand for the Divine Spark, the latter for the seed-atom. For all practical purposes we could say they stand for the outer and inner aspects of the seed-atom respectively.

This supernal Eros is far removed from the popular conception which identifies him with Cupid. He represents here the essence of Man which is Eros plus Anteros and springs from the Cosmic Egg like the philosophic concept of that Eros who was one of the earliest Greek gods. This cosmogonic Eros was the earliest force bringing order out of Chaos and he presided at the Council of the Gods and rules over the minds of gods and men: he was one of the gods of the Samothracian Mysteries.

**14**

The star Sirius has always been held in esoteric teaching to have much influence on Solar evolution. Astronomically speaking, of course, the position in space of Sirius is far outside the solar system but from a Cosmic standpoint Sirius and many other stars 'condition' the Solar Logos and, since the Solar Logos is Itself Conditioner of and conditioned by Its universe, the influences of Sirius and other stars are transmuted correspondingly before being communicated to the universe. Therefore, in the purely esoteric sense, stars in general and Sirius in particular (because of its special influence) can be considered in relation to Solar evolution—more especially those which, like Sirius, have had a marked effect on it. The individual, however, must have completed the cycle of Solar development before he can experience the *pure* influence of Sirius or other stars.

**15**

Orthodox science studies the materials of which the body of the earth is made and their composition, but the 'deeps' of the Inner Earth, the make-up of the Planetary Being is what is most important to esoteric studies. It can be helpful to think of the earth rather as a planet, a globe in the Solar system than as 'the world' and a development brought about by many civilizations to one of which we now belong. That which sustained and nurtured those civilizations is the Planetary Being. This tremendous force is sometimes personalized as 'The Earth Mother', but, personalization or no, all should be aware of the gigantic force involved and of how they are beholden to it. The Archangelic Guide assigned to the Planetary Being might be considered to supply higher aspects to it corresponding to the 'Intellectual Principle' in man. The names of these Archangelic Guides as known traditionally can be found in standard works of reference such as *The Mystical Qabalah*.

## 16

Each planet has within it the principles of a universe (as indeed has the atom) so that the Group soul of the planet's life comes through in aspects somewhat analogous to the Three Aspects of the Logos. There is something of the Aspect of 'Love', of 'Wisdom' and of 'Power' in each planet. Planets have had their 'Leaders' who have shown forth certain principles by their conditions of life even as there have been Teachers who did this for the guidance of mankind. These planetary aspects affected certain sections of the human race for they affected the Life-Swarms as they came down. Thus according to the aspects prevalent on certain planets which were in contact with man as he then was so did a particular Swarm receive a conditioning.

These great 'stresses of planetary substance' have much influence both in their own sphere and on the Earth because when the Earth was, so to speak, beginning its course in the heavens various influences and substances from different planets penetrated the then empty and uncoordinated mass which became the Earth: these stresses have left their mark on the Earth's structure and innermost nature and account sometimes for disturbances of one kind or another—earthquakes, for example, for there is still a link between certain substances in the Earth and the corresponding substance in some other planet and the two activate each other and reactions are set up in both. That is largely the basis of the more accurate side of astrology, but it is too intricate and too remote for most today to study deeply or use as a basis of assessment.

In very early days the most advanced among the priesthood knew about the stellar and planetary 'stresses' and the Earth's magnetism and on that knowledge built a system of which, indeed, something remains though the bases of the system have been forgotten. There are people on the Earth whose psychic faculty can be stirred by such stresses; some people, for example, are sensitive to earthquakes or atmospheric pressures in a way others are not. Such people have in their inner make-up some of the stresses corresponding to those of the particular planet which is disturbing the Earth. Certain planets influence the 'Water', 'Fire', 'Air' and 'Earth' conditions of the Earth by acting on the Earth's aura.

The underlying principle is that of the unity of all. The Earth is not unique; it should be considered for what it is—one of the bodies in the Solar System which has passed through states and conditions which have gradually condensed into what we call the 'Earth' but which have passed down from the Moon, Venus, Saturn and other planets.

The Planetary Beings can be considered in one way as the Group Souls of the planets and may be given by the visual imagination a definite form—as indeed in ancient days was done. Out of these Planetary Beings as they affected the mind and character of man were later evolved by vision and imagination into astral forms the forces known to mythology. There is, therefore, a strong link between Planetary Beings and the appropriate god-forms as is studied by some even today.

At the end of evolutions planets change over and different planets go into action during the succeeding evolution so that the subject of astrology at the present day has to contend with difficulties that are practically insurmountable.

There is much to be learnt about the Life-Swarms and the way in which their coming down affects humanity generally in the present. All those ancient happenings and developments must be included in any estimation of the condition of man and his development. During the various historical periods certain Planetary Forces—for Planetary Forces is a more accurate description than 'Planets'—influenced the Earth, each according to its special nature; when these Forces are brought to bear again in their turn they bring to the surface conditions corresponding to their nature, they bring them about in the Earth. Although we have used the term 'Planetary Forces' we include also certain Stellar Forces working through the Solar Jurisdiction, such as the Signs of the Zodiac, but that subject is too vast to be dealt with in detail now. Bear in mind, however, the Sign of Gemini, for the Forces signified by that Sign influenced Atlantis and will influence Earth again later in the present age. The stars are set in configurations somewhat similar to those which influenced the last days of Atlantis: certain major Planetary Forces and Signs are influencing mankind again and though the combinations are different there is something of the same kind of inner condition: the combinations are different but there is something of a similar inner condition and the world, though not deluged by a water cataclysm, is full of clashes and strife of various kinds.

## 17

Let us consider the Second Swarm, the life-wave of those great Regents of the Logos we call the 'Lords of Form'. They might also be called the 'Builders' for through them all form, all shape is developed. The shape that covers or encases the life-consciousness is made by the builders to hold that life for a time sufficient for the life to react as needed to the stresses of the Sphere on which it is after which the life withdraws to another condition leaving the form to decompose into the elements of the Sphere. This is one of the earliest conceptions of 'death', so that the Lords of Form are also the 'Gods of Death'.

Where there is death on a large scale, especially death on a group scale as in war, the Lords of Form are intimately concerned for then the whole planet is as it were shaken and its planetary forces need reconstruction. The Lords of Form work with group souls more than with individuals but where a great teacher is instructing mankind (especially if the teaching concerns human evolution) the Lords of Form are at work adapting the 'planetary matter' to the new and greater concept of life and evolution being brought through. When The Christ using the body of Jesus of Nazareth, strongly influenced the planet Earth there were very definite though perhaps incalculable changes in the actual lines of the Earth: these were not observable by science perhaps but the Logoidal Forces change to another course so to speak and the inner forces behind the outer manifestation of the Earth—the etheric structure—began to alter. Form is not confined to outline but is essentially the whole shape and fills the need of Life for a particular shape: the shape does not appear all at once but grows and develops in the course of evolution, as indeed does the life.

The actual outlines or configurations of Cosmic form such as the stars, planets, and large land masses are all influenced by the Lords of Form. The ancients were aware of these very early beings (the Lords of Form) and their powers, recognizing them as great Titanic Forces much connected with fire and metallic ores and paying homage to them in some of the earliest Mysteries.

These Lords are behind the great chemical (and alchemical) fires. They construct shape by means of mingling and uniting the Elemental Powers and the metallic and mineral forces of the Earth—building structures of every kind especially planetary structures for they it was who built the planets. You will notice that the larger and vaster forms are always the simplest—the great spherical forms are the simplest but smaller types increase in complexity, as a comparision of the huge prehistoric animals with the present-day fauna will show. The 'outer' structure of a planet is indeed simple.

The Lords of Form may also be called the 'Lords of Rhythm' (just as the Lords of Flame may be called the 'Lords of Vibration') because of their rhythmical advance and retreat in the building of the universe. That was the beginning of rhythm in the universe and it set the great rhythms 'Death' and 'Birth'. Thus can these Lords be called the 'Lords of Death' and they are deeply connected with the Ring-Chaos; they have the great driving force of reaction that will finally break up a form and release the force. They are at work behind the construction of mineral forms for these are after-developments of the form of the Earth and the life of the planet is within the mineral in a certain way.

All the ancient legends of the great Powers of the Underworld—the chthonic Forces of Hammer and Anvil, the hammering into shape of great streams of force, the Blacksmith Gods, deal with the Builders and lesser types of Elemental beings concerned with work as servants of the Lords of Form. In a properly worked ritual the Elemental beings build certain forms on the astral which hold together the stresses of force until other forces take over: rhythm or repetition is important here for the frequent building of the forms eventually makes it as near 'solid' as is possible on the astral plane. Just as the efficient and 'contacted' occultist makes use of the service and co-operation of these Builders so, on a much larger scale, did the Logos use the powers of the Lords of Form to construct not only the Earth but also the other planets of Its system. All the solar system is interlinked and reflections of the attributes of other planets will be seen within certain mineral forms of the Earth—certain precious stones, for instance, are very closely connected with other planets and this connection is not based only on superstition. Similarly certain metals have a composition which links them to certain basic outlines and substances of other planets giving not only an analogy with them but also a certain definite linking.

An imaginative picture of these great Lords of Form could be made by visualizing a vast amphitheatre under the earth in darkness filled with red flashes from the depths of inner earth. Through this darkness can be heard a hammer on an anvil—very faintly at first for it is very remote. Imagine this sound as coming gradually nearer with a tremendous rhythm, hard, strong, simple. As that rhythmic sound increases in intensity giant forms gradually begin to build in outline—vast forms dimly and only partly seen in outline for they are too huge and too strong to be contained in space as we know it; feel the etheric intensification 'behind' the dimly discerned form.

Within this work which is being done by the Lords of Form is a vast patience which is content to take millions of years over the task it has set itself so that it can be perfectly done. Every time the Great Worker returns to a task he brings a new power derived from the Logos and from the Sphere in which he accomplished his last work, and this new power gives a somewhat changed type of force to the work. And ever the great hammer beats and beats and beats through Time—building, unbuilding and building again: such are the great Regents of the Logos entrusted with this work.

These Regents are also the servers of the Aspect of the Logos behind death, and regeneration and rebuilding. We can invoke the Lords of Form to help us to earn our freedom from form when the time approaches. He who knows and understands death has already overcome it—he is a pupil of the Lords of Form. We would do well to give a thought to the great Builders who have built us and the planetary spheres and who are behind the laws of shape whether on the astral or physical plane, with whom we can co-operate as agents of the Divine.

## 18

In *The Mystical Qabalah* there are references to the Archangels of the Ten Holy Sephiroth. These are the 'Intelligences' of the Spheres and are of the First Swarm—Lords of Flame. That Intelligence works with the archetypal force of the Sphere and under its control are the 'Angels of the Sphere' which execute the wishes of the Archangels according to their natures.

The Sphere of Malkuth comprises the mundane plane and the spiritual values which are immediately within dense matter—in fact the 'Spirit of the Atom'—and it is under the aegis of the Lord of the Four Elements we call Sandalphon. This Archangel is one to be invoked by those especially who find difficulty in coming to grips with the physical plane, for it is he who has charge of the 'soul' of physical objects. If you could see with your physical vision the exact inner plane condition of a chair or a table you would observe a very slow vibration and movement of infinite numbers of tiny 'molecules' holding together the dense matter. Sandalphon is the Overlord of all these activities. Those who are so inclined can visualize a great angelic form in the four Qabalistic colours of Malkuth—pale yellow, olive green, russet and black; his vibrationary rate is slow and somewhat ponderous for it belongs to the plane of dense matter and the connecting link of etheric just behind that plane.

The Sphere of Yesod concerns among other things the deeper and remoter etheric substance—the Akasha as it is sometimes called—and here the Archangel is that known as Gabriel, ruler of many subtle realms in nature and in man. He is the Lord of Dreams and of the subtle vibrations of a rare kind which can touch the clairvoyant faculties of man. In Christianity he is associated with the Annunciation partly because he is 'The Mystic Announcer'—the controller of a special kind of message which can reach to the human mind from far-off planes; he is, in fact, the Angel of Annunciation to many others than Mary. Thus he is also concerned with sleep—that condition in which the dense body is inactive and subtle vehicles can escape from it to other planes. It is a large part of his work to induce what is a part of 'the Moon Consciousness' in man; he tends to draw the soul magnetically even as a great water power draws and therefore his influence is a kind of sedative on the physical power—he draws the consciousness from it. He may be pictured as a huge ovoid of silvery substance with the delicate lilac and violet of Yesod in his 'wings' and the sound of mighty waters which show his special type of vibration.

The Sphere of Tiphareth is presided over by the Archangel Raphael. He holds the healing and sustaining powers of sunlight—especially is he concerned with the modern methods of radiant heat and infra-red and ultra-violet rays, though these are as yet from the esoteric standpoint only in their infancy.

Finally, there is the Sphere of Kether whose Archangel is Metatron. He is said to have been responsible for the symbol of the Tree of Life's being given to man. He works in the great world of Cosmic Archetypes, and his influence is very rare. It is of the type that comes as a blinding flash of illumination of remote spiritual truths.

Thus far we have dealt with the Sephiroth on the Middle Pillar of the composite symbol of the Tree of Life and the Pillars. Let us now consider the Sephiroth on the two Side Pillars.

The Archangel of the Sphere of Chokmah is Ratziel. He brought through the creative forces in early evolution. it is difficult to formulate in the human mind such beings as either Metatron (of Kether) or Ratziel, for they are beyond form as we know it, and also are incapable of being 'reduced' to a symbol in any way adequate save perhaps that of great 'Pillars of Glory' with no fixed outlines.

The Archangel of the Sphere of Binah—Tzaphkiel—has been behind the formulation of all the mystic cults that have been sent down from time to time by the Inner Plane Adepti. He is the 'Archangel of the Temple' and can be envisaged as a vast Presence shining with a certain living darkness with a wonderful rose-coloured glow in the centre.

The Archangel of Chesed—Tzadkiel—has a great influence giving an assurance of benevolence and the utter calm of eternal security and certainty. He could be of great help to any who are prone to irritation or unbalance of temper.

The Archangel of Geburah—Khamael—is the Protector of the weak and wronged; he is also the Avenging Angel who punishes the breakers of Law.

The Archangel of Netzach—Haniel—is the Archangel of the Sphere of harmony and beauty, and especially of inter-relationships whether of Spheres, planets, plants or animal and human life: the great archetype of sympathetic vibration. He can be visualized as shining with a green and golden flame and with a rose-coloured light over his head.

The Archangel of Hod is Michael. Hod is the Sphere of 'magic', and Michael is its Archangel because he holds in control the various evil influences which might escape into the world of men. He is thus a very essential protector in 'magical formulae'—especially where the would-be practitioners are inexperienced. The ancient Jews listed whole choirs of angels by name in addition to the great beings here enumerated, and to deal with them would require much time; but you have here some indications about ten so great that they are—each in his own Sphere—in charge of the mighty Emanations of God. Many who 'work the Tree' are inclined to try to get into touch with the God-Forces of the Sephiroth (using the god-forms of varying pantheons) whereas, in fact, there are certain archetypal powers of these Spheres that are better brought through by use of the Archangelic powers and forms.

## 19

The teaching on the Ray Exemplars—especially that contained in Chapter 20—is of great importance and should be carefully meditated upon. The teaching has been given in a very condensed form—largely owing to the abstruse and difficult nature of the subject which made it very difficult to put the ideas into adequate expression in language. A good way to obtain an understanding is to think of the great Teachers and Redeemers of mankind who have guided the various phases of evolution in all conditions—both Cosmic and mundane.

Think of the mighty influences and 'conditions' that pour through the great currents of force marked by the Zodiacs—the Greater Zodiac of the Rays, and the better-known Lesser Zodiac. In these great currents work various types of the Redemptive Force of the Logos, or, to use a more Cosmic phrase, the great Cosmic Force fuses in a special way on a special occasion with what might be called the central aspect of the Logos in order the better to influence evolution. As the different types of this great Force touch our own evolution they give off to each one a definite influence—they act as nourishers, helpers, feeders of that particular Divine Spark. So it has always been in every phase of our evolution.

The Being of whom we know most is he who is sometimes called 'The Lord of the Purple Ray'. He is, so to speak, the 'group-mind' of that Ray—a great group-mind which is at the super-phase in which it leads on our evolution to its conclusion. The tremendous force of which I speak—the 'Anointed Force' of the Purple Ray—has focused to some extent from time to time in some great Guide or Leader who has come down into the world of men, but the Lord of the Purple Ray is, of course, unique.

The intricacy of the subject makes it nearly impossible to give a clear exposition in words alone; words should be combined with deep contemplation and concentration rather than with only intellectual meditation to gain some beginning of understanding which will continue to grow. The names and attributes traditionally given to the Ray Exemplars are of high importance, not only because they give some idea of the Being through whom the force focused in this world, but because they can put you in touch with a Cosmic power which exceeds the force of the Ray shown when their bearers were in the world. There is, naturally, a difference between the 'Cosmic Christ' and the Force of the Cosmic Christ focused in an individual, but the latter proceeds from the former and could not manifest without it.

The forces of the Ray Exemplars are very strong and very deep. It can be of great value to link them mentally with those more abstract aspects of the individual called variously in esotericism the 'Higher Self' or the Individuality.

It is possible in suitably prepared conditions for this great Force to be contacted in ritual but great care is needed as it can have a destructive effect in 'burning up the dross' if it is brought too near the earth-plane. Normally in ritualistic conditions it acts—to use the symbolism of the Qabalistic Tree of Life—from the Supernal Triangle through Tiphareth and does not come 'below' that Sephirah but on occasion it may work through to the astral and etheric levels using a group of people as a basis of manifestation and bringing about repercussions whereby all in that group would be affected since none could be in contact with such a Force and remain unaffected. The great 'Ray' impinges on the Higher Self in such a manner as to impel it towards integration with the Personality, and everyone save those whose integration was well advanced would feel strong effects which might well be beyond their capacity at that stage to support. When this 'Ray' is brought through the Personality has to absorb in a way the experience of the Higher Self even as the Higher Self has to absorb the experiences of the Personality after physical death.

This power of the Cosmic Christ can be thought of as that of the higher planes of 'the Sun-behind-the-sun' which so to speak unites the Ray with the Logos. The time has now come when the great Force as a whole will no longer focus in a single being but in a group—ever widening until it takes in the whole world. The inner plane 'body' now used by the Force can be thought of as something like the highest esoteric conception of Horus. Nevertheless the beings in whom the Force once manifested individually still work in remote planes and maintain in the Cosmos the distinctive power with which they once worked on earth.

It is sometimes liable to cause confusion if a 'Ray' is associated with a special colour. The 'Ray' of the Cosmic Christ is that of the Oversoul of the Lords of Mind. It works through the precessional Signs of the Zodiac and contains within itself a whole spectrum or a set of strata of colours of which strata the so-called 'Purple Ray' is a stratum. The Green Ray or green stratum of the same great Ray worked through the force described in the legends of Osiris, Orpheus and Dionysos. It is the true Ray of Mind and leads to the innermost sanctuaries of the 'Mysteries'.

## 20

Man's primal loyalty is to the One—Unity. 'Loyalty' is hardly the correct word to use as the One is a Law—no other type of existence is possible; in It we live and move and have our being. It is, however, very necessary to understand that the One—the Logos—is actually the becoming manifest of the Unmanifest; It is Unity not because It is concentrated or limited but because It is undifferentiated.

The nucleus of the being of each immortal soul is a 'nucleus of energy' in the Unmanifest. The Logos provides the ordered substance of manifestation on all planes whence we built up the vehicles of manifestation on each plane. Therefore is our manifested existence conditioned thereby, the Logoidal nature being the law of existence to which we must submit if we would live harmoniously in manifestation. The nucleus of each living soul does not derive its existence from the Logoidal Being but from the Unmanifest Itself. However, as man manifests forth in the sphere of the Solar Logos man must work in and through its conditions which are the laws of the Logoidal nature. The Solar Logos is the God of the Solar System and gives it its laws; this Logos, working through the Planetary Beings and their Archangelic Guides is the source of the differentiated energy manifesting within the bounds of the solar nebula. In brief, the Solar Logos is the Conditioner and Sustainer of manifestation in Its universe: the Great Unmanifest is unconditioned.

**21**

There are three titles which might be confusing unless a clear idea of the way in which they are used has been gained. They are (1) the Planetary Entity, (2) the Planetary Intelligence or the Archangelic Intelligence, (3) the Planetary Being.

The Planetary Entity is the Logoidal Idea of the 'planet' as it is to become in its spiritual sense at the end of evolution. The concept of this has many symbolic descriptions, such as 'The Kingdom,' 'The New Jerusalem,' etc.

The Planetary Intelligence or the Archangelic Intelligence is the Archangel appointed to guide the 'planet' during its evolution; that Archangel is one of the First Swarm. That assigned to earth is known in the West as Sandalphon. He is said to have first come into close control of earth during the Lemurian Period when Fire was in a particular manner being introduced into earth. This Archangel, great as he is, is said to be not quite of the stature of the Planetary Intelligence of Venus or Mercury; from our present viewpoint, however, his greatness is such that the distinction to us is largely academic. He, too, is developing and reaching out, so to speak, towards another great Force—and this concept is indicated in certain esoteric allegories dealing with the symbolism of marriages. From time to time great entities from other and more developed 'planets' have been in touch with Sandalphon's planetary work, especially from the planet Venus.

The Planetary Being is as it were a vast Elemental composed of the consciousness (using the word in a wide sense) of each one of its children—the children being all the lives upon the earth, humans, beasts, birds, reptiles, fish, insects, etc. In the great Elemental, the Planetary Being, all these are, or should be, one: and so they are, or should be, one in their relationship to each other; it is because that relationship has been shaken, broken and betrayed that so many ills have come to pass. It can be assumed that when 'the Kingdom comes,' when the Logoidal Idea of this planet is truly manifested then indeed all earth-creatures will be one on a certain level.

All should remember that as developed and developing human beings they have a great debt to the earth who is in very truth their mother, their parent; they are made of her substance and live upon her substance and all that they do here on earth, all that they discover in science, all that they make in art or industry are also parts of her. But she develops less quickly than her children and it is the duty of the children by their development to aid hers. Therefore, whatsoever you do let it be not only for your own gain or interest but also for the gain and keen interest of the Planetary Being. The more that you do that is consciously shared with this vast Elemental parent the more will those things prosper not only in her but in you. There is no thing on earth, no thought brought through to earth which does not concern the Planetary Being—however great or lofty, however (unfortunately) mean or base. You have a very great responsibility not only to yourselves and to each other but also to the great group-soul of the earth, the great mass-mother of you all.

The more you are in touch with her the more will you earn the privilege of the contact with her Guiding Intelligence and that Intelligence will guide you, too, not only in matters immediately concerning the earth-life but in using such things to pave the way for the future towards the time when the Planetary Being will become one with the Planetary Entity. Therefore, help to join these two together—the Logoidal Concept of the earth (which even if you cannot clearly envisage it you can to some extent imagine) and the Planetary Being; and let that purpose unite with your wish to forward evolution and your effort to pass on all that you can of help to the earth-mother. As all of you develop through the Ages so do you carry this vast parent and her development along with you. When you stray from the right path so do you lead her astray and this is a grievous wrong for it holds the degradation of the Planetary Being.

Be mindful, too, in thinking of the Planetary Being to think also of all other stages of life upon her—birds, beasts, insects, Elements and all forms of life for to these do you bear relationship. There has been much superstition and sentimentality connected with this Divine Law of Unity but keep well in mind the great truth of the interrelationship of all when you shed the superstition.

Be aware of the Planetary Being as a being of immense age in which each one of you is as it were embedded and through which you draw your earth-life; it could be compared to an enormous bee-hive with millions of sections each of which holds a small bee making honey. Be aware, too, of the Archangelic Intelligence as having tremendous protection, love and devotion for each and every creature on the earth because each creature is part of earth and as being able to guide each one of you either indirectly through the Planetary Being or directly if you have the right approach to him and have earned and maintained the right of direct contact with him.

What is said here, however fanciful the expression may appear, is deeply real and worth the intensest consideration.

# Index